IT'S A WOMAN'S WORLD

RUTH STOUT

Martino Fine Books
Eastford, CT
2018

Martino Fine Books
P.O. Box 913,
Eastford, CT 06242 USA

ISBN 978-1-68422-241-4

Cover Design Tiziana Matarazzo

Printed in the United States of America On 100% Acid-Free Paper

IT'S A WOMAN'S WORLD

RUTH STOUT

DOUBLEDAY & COMPANY, INC., GARDEN CITY, N.Y. 1960

Printed in the United States of America

for Virginia,
who doesn't need it

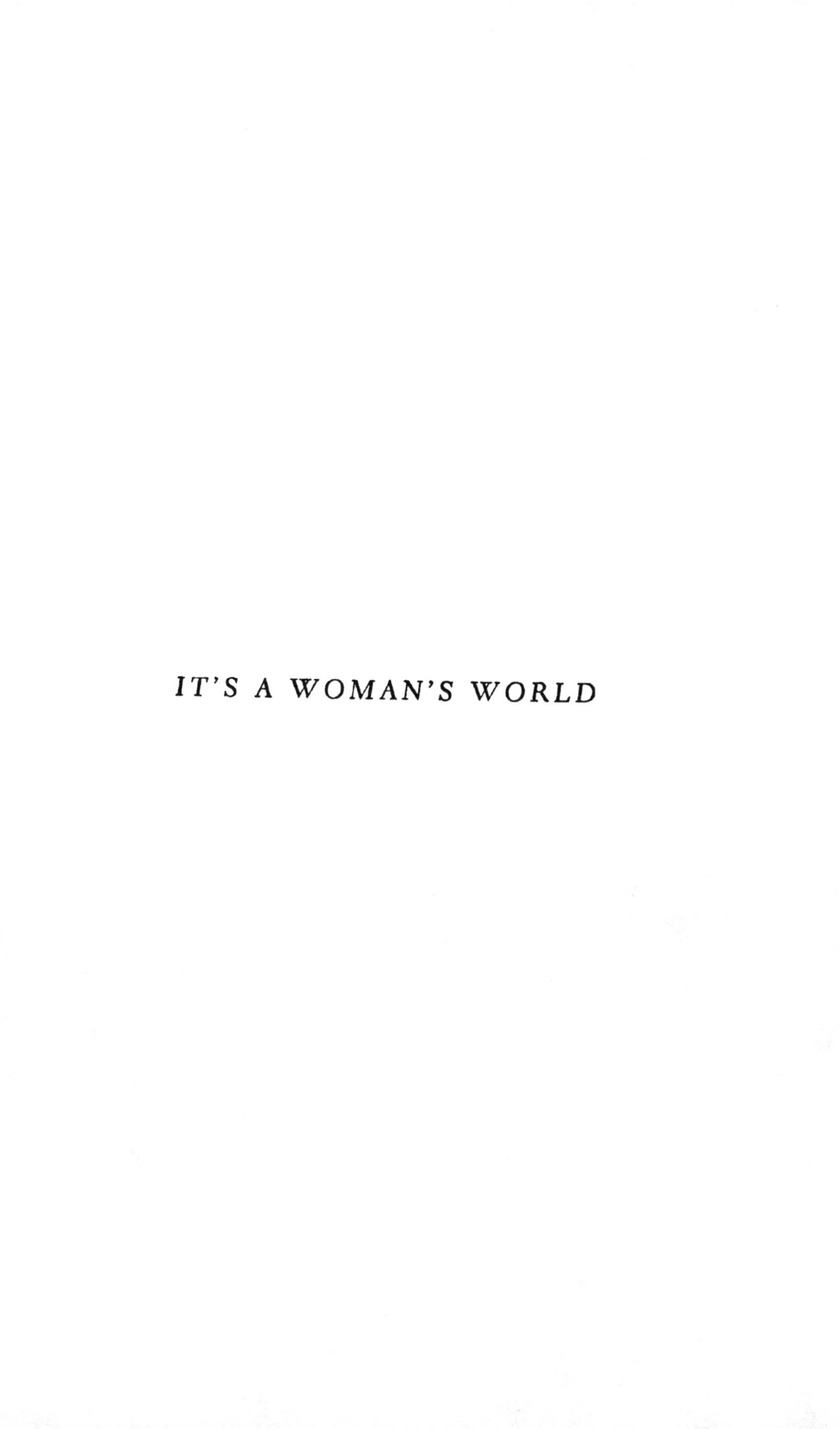

IT'S A WOMAN'S WORLD

I

The Right Window

Among the theories that various people are busy thinking up is the proposition that suffering and frustration are beneficial in the long run, that they strengthen our characters, improve our souls, and may eventually get us into heaven. That's a helpful attitude to take if we are miserable over something beyond our control, such as a broken leg, a slump in the stock market, a rainy day.

However, I doubt if many of us would deliberately set out to suffer purely for the benefit we hoped to derive from it; for instance, I can't visualize anyone putting something bitter into the stew in order to make stoics of the various members of the family. It sounds ridiculous, yet it is only slightly less so than the fact that so many women today voluntarily fill their lives with complications and activities which they would be happier without and about which they keep on complaining. On all sides one sees and hears of women who are discontented, hectic, frustrated, and yet the truth of the matter is that in many respects they don't need to be.

One Sunday at breakfast with my husband, Fred, and a friend who was spending the weekend with us, the two men got to arguing about who led a more frenzied life, a mother of half a dozen children or a career woman, and Joe turned to me and asked, "Why don't you write a book telling women what-for?"

"Why, I would be glad to," I replied, thinking he was joking.

But it turned out that he wasn't, and Fred abetted him. They insisted that if a woman enjoyed her life as much as I enjoyed mine she was a rather selfish specimen if she wasn't willing to try to share her secret.

Well, I hadn't realized that I had a secret. Moreover, the job of telling people how you manage your life, with the idea they might learn something of value, is a big one. And presumptuous besides. But, urged to give the matter some thought, I have come up with a few answers.

I remember one afternoon when, as a child, I was gazing out of our dining room window at my two elder brothers in the distance. Their dog had just been run over in the road and they were burying it under a big oak tree. I really hadn't cared much for the animal but I knew that Bob had loved it beyond anything, so the tears were running down my cheeks.

Just then my grandfather called me; he said he wanted to show me something. And there, through another window, I saw three buds opening on my own private rosebush. As I turned to run outside to get a closer look at the flowers, and to smell them, my grandfather put his hand under my chin and said, with his wise blue eyes full of meaning, "Thee was looking through the wrong window."

Without a sermon, without a lot of talk, I wish that every youngster could have it impressed on him that nothing forces him to dwell on the thing that disturbs him, when right at hand there may be something that could lift his spirit. It's good to realize this when we're young, but I don't believe it is too late at any age to make it a part of one's philosophy and, better still, a daily habit.

I think I was quite young when I figured out that there was no sense in doing anything unless you had a reason for it. Once at school I told a fib of some sort, and the teacher told me I must stay in at recess and write "I will never again tell a lie" on the blackboard fifty times. I wrote the words three times, then I said to myself, this is silly; these words themselves are a lie because if I don't die pretty quick I surely will tell another fib sometime.

I explained this to the teacher but he thought I should complete the writing, and we spent the rest of recess arguing about it. I tried my best to make him understand that writing that promise over and over couldn't make a particle of difference in my future telling of lies and was therefore a waste of time. If he wanted to punish me, why didn't he made me wash the windows or do something else that would be of some use?

It seems to me that I always hated waste, particularly of time, because no matter how hard you figured, there was never enough of that for doing all the things you could think up.

Nor do I like competition and I know just how and when I got *that* way. As a child, I felt I had to excel; if I couldn't be the best in anything I wanted no part of it. But being stubborn and having a lot of endurance, I managed to come through with a reasonable share of honors.

I must have been about ten years old when we bought a croquet set, and I grew to love the game and often played with my sister, Juanita, two years older than I, and my brother Rex, two years my junior. It wasn't much fun to play with Juanita because she was a casual player and didn't care whether she won or not, but Rex and I were evenly matched and it was a triumph to beat him. And I could just barely stand it when he won.

One day when he beat me I wandered into the house, thinking it didn't matter much whether I lived or died; with one glance at me, Mother knew that my world had come to an end, and she asked, "Did Rex win?"

I nodded, not trusting myself to speak, and Mother continued, "Well, tomorrow maybe you'll beat him and then *he* will be miserable."

A wise woman, she knew exactly the right time to plant a seed. From that day on I still of course preferred to win at croquet, but the thrill of it, tempered with another's despair, and the agony at losing were both gone. In any competition, unless it's a tie, somebody has to pay in defeat for what another gains in success. It has been a long time since I have been able to enjoy an accomplishment through somebody else's failure.

Making too much out of too little is a pathetic and almost universal pastime; I remember an exaggerated instance of this when I had a tearoom in Greenwich Village many years ago. One of my daily customers was a super-sensitive artist. His chief occupation and actually his greatest pride was suffering; he felt you couldn't amount to much if you didn't suffer fairly constantly and by all means acutely. One day he came into my place in a state of shock, and I thought that surely this time something worth getting upset about had happened to him. But it turned out that he had seen a woman in a department store buying ribbon to match a sample of some material, and the color she was choosing outraged him to such an extent that he had done his best to persuade her to get another shade of ribbon, but to no avail.

Now many people have a strong feeling about colors, and I must confess that some combinations I've seen have made me wince a little, but I think you are just indulging yourself if you let such a thing spoil your day.

A friend of mine who had taken a job as a salad maker in a high-class restaurant told me the following: there were two kinds of salads served which included tomatoes; in one kind the tomato was sliced and in the other it was quartered. My friend got confused and put slices on a salad which should have had quarters, and the young woman who inspected the food just before it was taken into the dining room came close to having hysterics when she saw this mistake. My friend was so disgusted that she quit the job on the spot.

These two incidents are extremes, but one of the hardest things to learn is not to mind inconsequential mishaps. I have had to work hard at this and of course haven't conquered it completely, but I do improve. All we need is a little common sense. Will this really matter in twenty-four hours? I ask myself. The answer is usually No, but if it's Yes, then I shove the time ahead: day after tomorrow, next week, next month. Almost anything with a time limit can be taken philosophically.

Worry and remorse come under this same category as far as their futility goes; these make no sense and there is no possibility of any constructive results. If you will force yourself to live in the moment, to avoid the wrong window, you should be able to conquer worry.

As for remorse, if we have treated someone badly and are truly sorry for our actions, which are beyond remedying, then surely the only sensible procedure is to try to do better in the future. If we mope around, spending the days in bitter regret that we have failed someone in the past, we may at that very time be failing someone else who may badly need us to snap out of it and be more cheerful.

Some years ago an Englishman stayed with us for about ten months; he had been everything from a panhandler up—or down—and was a law unto himself. He told us that only once had anyone had the nerve to tell him that he *had* to do something, and he had replied, "Listen, brother, there's only one thing that I've *got* to do, and that's die."

And it's surprising how nearly right he was. To a less extravagant degree I had adopted that attitude by the time I'd reached my late twenties; if anything at all arose which I didn't want to do, or accept, I would ask myself, do I have to stand for this? Usually I didn't.

I happened to learn this lesson because at the time there was a good deal for me to either stand for or rebel against. About half of our family had landed in New York without money or jobs, and my brother Rex decided to be a bookkeeper and insisted that I do the same, since most other office jobs for girls paid meager salaries. I knew nothing whatever about bookkeeping but Rex said Never mind about that; whenever I came to a snag I could ask him what to do. Both of us ignored the fact that he had never studied bookkeeping either.

I was somewhat wary of the whole idea, but Rex was always a first-class persuader, so I got a job with Franklin Simon and Company as a ledger clerk. After a few months I was promoted to head bookkeeper of the wholesale department, and being too diffident to admit how little I knew about the whole affair, I floundered along, learning as I went, and kept the job seven years. Every time the office manager called my attention to some blunder I had made, I would say sincerely, "I think I had better go back and be a ledger clerk"; then he would give me some unearned praise and insist that I go on as I was.

The work was hard, even if you knew what you were doing; the store was growing very rapidly and after a few years my department had a staff of eleven girls. I had started with three.

During the busy seasons several of us in my office often worked overtime at night, and in those days there was no such thing as being paid for extra work. The regular daily hours were long enough, 8:30 to 6:00. When the work was slack I decided to let my girls take turns coming in late and going home early, or having an afternoon or a day off. This seemed fair to me, considering how cheerfully they worked overtime when the work was heavy. Even if they hadn't been pleasant about doing extra time, I would have felt they had earned some hours off.

We didn't punch a clock, but everybody had to pass a timekeeper in the morning and evening, and the first time we received our pay envelopes after I had begun to give the girls some free hours, their salaries had all been adjusted accordingly. I asked myself, do I have to stand for this? The answer seemed to me to be No.

Taking the pay envelopes with me I went in to the office manager and told him I would like to know which was the policy and pleasure of the store: to have the employees in my office present each day from exactly 8:30 to 6 o'clock or to have the work done. Whichever it was, my girls would be glad to cooperate; through the slack seasons they would come in full time every day and sit there, whether there was any work to do or not, if that was what the store wanted, and it would of course naturally follow that we would work the same hours in the busy seasons, never mind that the work wouldn't get finished.

I won, of course; the poor devil had no choice, for the work really piled up at the busy times of year. And it probably wasn't feasible for him to hire a larger year-round staff, or to get in temporary help when the work was so heavy.

The office manager was a huge man, a Greek, whose name was Alexander Maurocordato (he had shortened the latter to Mauro); he had piercing black eyes and an unbelievably aggressive beard. We all liked him, but he had a bad habit of coming into our office and just standing and sort of glaring around, which made the girls nervous.

I decided that we didn't have to put up with this, so every time he wandered in, I would ask him for a raise for one of the girls, and it wasn't long before he was avoiding our department as one would the plague.

My office became a little independent kingdom. We got the work done on time, and correctly, but beyond that, we did exactly as we pleased. The senior partner of the firm, Mr. Florsheim, hated our lack of conformity. One afternoon, when we were having a gay party with cake and coffee, he came by, glanced in, couldn't bear it and with a scowl asked one of the girls what was going on. She replied with enthusiasm, "It's Phoebe's birthday."

"Always somesing in ziss office," the poor fellow muttered, disgusted but helpless.

It wasn't surprising that he, and the other bosses, didn't interfere with us; they obviously sensed something which was a settled fact, although my staff and I had never discussed it. It was just this: we stood together and we knew our power. What did surprise me was that although all of the other departments in the store were very envious of us, none of them made any attempt to emulate us.

This experience, among others, taught me that it's a mistake to submit to something you don't approve of, unless you are very sure you can do nothing about it. However, the main thing, which covers all the rest, is to do your own thinking; it may not be really first-class but at least it will be your own.

This above all: to thine own self be true,
And it must follow, as the night the day,
Thou canst not then be false to any man.

That, from Shakespeare, has helped me ever since I was a little girl and my oldest sister, May, told me about it; much later I discovered Montaigne's "The greatest thing in the world is to learn to belong to yourself."

This is easier than you might believe, once you give it some thought and decide that it is what you really want. However, it is essential that you be honest with yourself, and that takes some doing.

What do you want from yourself? Respect? Then hold up

your head, throw back your shoulders, and stand on your own feet.

And what do you want from others? Also respect, perhaps, and liking? Then be yourself, for you surely want your friends to like the real you, not just an unreasonable facsimile of Mrs. Tom or Mrs. Dick or Mrs. Harry.

"Lead thy captivity captive." Think how much more profound that is than "Lead thy captor captive." For the slave isn't told to overpower his master, the man in jail isn't advised to somehow break out. No, you can be a slave or a prisoner, but if you can rise above your condition, perhaps even use it and learn from it, you are free. It isn't others nor iron bars that we have to conquer or learn to control; it is ourselves. Putting it into as few words as possible, I'd say that one road to happiness for women—and for men too—boils down to knowing yourself and thinking for yourself, with a minimum of conflict and inconsistency between your pretensions and your performance.

Now I realize, of course, that if we all did our own thinking our economic system might collapse almost overnight, but, as far as we know, it might be a good thing if it did; we would be compelled to think up something else and the new regime might even be sensible. We might ask ourselves, for instance, what this standard of living which we glibly boast about is based on, and we would have to reply, on money, on material possessions. We might ponder the fact that our mental hospitals are overflowing, and that our children cheer when the movie or T.V. hero rips open his enemy with a knife. ("Love your enemies"—remember?) Why should a boy who hears adults talk of killing their enemies by the millions with atom bombs think it's wrong to go after just one with a knife? It's bad enough when we don't do our own thinking; it's almost criminal to do so little toward helping children to figure things out for themselves.

Recently I attended a meeting of the Pen Women's Club, which had asked me to give a talk. At lunch before the meeting I put out a few feelers, trying to find out what they would like to have me discuss.

A woman sitting next to me said something about teen-agers feeling that they simply had to conform, and she illustrated: her seventeen-year-old son had that morning suddenly refused to wear a shirt that he had always particularly liked, because the collar didn't button down; he had said that everyone was wearing shirts with buttoned collars now, and he wasn't going to wear any other kind.

I blurted out, "Well, of course that sort of reasoning is the fault of the boy's mother," and the woman muttered, "Oh dear!" and looked so pained that I hastened to add, "Perhaps not the individual mother but all of them in general."

How can I possibly be wrong about that? Let us start by admitting that we are living in a tense, violent, even possibly insane world, and let's sit back and listen while the women blame the men for all of it. Aren't they at the head of nations? Aren't they the ones who design and make guns and bombs? Wasn't it the men who got the bright idea of using the taxpayers' money to devise a way to reach the moon? And for what purpose except, perhaps, because they were afraid they might run out of enemies down here and wouldn't have any more targets for the deadly weapons they are manufacturing? What a let-down it would be if, when they got to the moon, they wouldn't find a single live thing to shoot at! It is men who set ridiculous, hard-to-wear feminine styles, but while they really put their minds to it when figuring out how to make a rocket, they can't make a durable pair of stockings. Perhaps, though, that last item is a matter of greed; maybe manufacturers don't want stockings to last very long.

So it's a man's world and women are helpless, innocent bystanders? Nonsense! Even if we had never heard that psychologists claim that the first few years of a person's life are the vital ones and to a great extent determine his character and future behavior, we surely could have figured out for ourselves that this must be true. Just as a baby learns a language word by word, and finds out that a pencil will make a mark on paper, and that a whistle will make a noise, he also discovers that Mamma has no backbone and will give in if he keeps after her, that she doesn't always tell the truth but goes into a tizzy if *he* tells a lie, that the only way to behave is to be a copycat, and that black children are not as good as white ones.

Can we get away from the fact that women (mothers, nurses, teachers) have almost complete control of men through the formative years? And also of the girls who will be the mothers and teachers of the next generation? This is a frightening responsibility. And it is also a strange state of affairs that the most far-reaching and important job in the world is undertaken as a matter of course by women who, for the most part, have had no special preparation for it. Perhaps it's beside the point that there really isn't anyone qualified to teach them.

A filing clerk has to know the alphabet, a stenographer has to know shorthand, even a radio announcer must, I suppose, have to know *something*, but a woman can become a mother and thereby undertake the most delicate, intricate, and exacting job possible without any study beforehand, or any skill, or even any liking for it. And, usually, she can't quit; she's stuck with the job and the unfortunate child is stuck with her.

Trying to build up her children's character and self-confidence isn't a mother's only job; the little ones must also be fed and clothed and kept out of mischief (not to mention entertained) and put to bed, eventually, thank goodness. A friend of mine once took exception to a remark I made to the effect that no matter how much parents loved their offspring, they seemed to look forward with longing to the tots' bedtime; she was indignant and accused me of disliking children. It happens that this woman not only has a cook but also a nurse, and so has very little conception of the *continuity* involved in the double job of housewife and mother.

And that is only part of the picture. Unlike the people (both men and women) who go off to a job every day, these homemakers seem to be forced to lead a life full of interruptions and demands. The telephone alone kills many precious minutes, and have you ever heard a telephone ring at a convenient time?

It's true that the woman who works in an office, or shop, or factory also has some clouds to her silver linings, and we will get around to that a little later on. But she can usually order her day to some extent and keep to her plans; she usually isn't definitely pushed now in this direction, now in that. And if she lives in a community where there are civic affairs and various drives for this or that cause, she usually isn't expected to be as active as the women who stay at home, because she "works."

But most women are confronted with problems, great and small, which fill their waking hours whether they like it or not, and at least a part of my purpose here is to try to point out that there are quite a lot of things we can do about it if we are fed up. We aren't helpless and we aren't robots; therefore it seems to me an excellent idea not to behave as though we were.

II

Live and Learn

If I were to be put in charge of running the world, I'm sure I would be tempted to abolish all sentences beginning with "If only. . . ." Almost any thought starting with these two words is likely to finish with something negative and futile and dead.

Can't you imagine how the "if onlys" would abound if there were such a thing as a wishing fairy? If only I had asked for this, not for that! Because, thank goodness, we do change and mature sufficiently to acquire new values.

When I was a little girl I would have had a hard time choosing between having my freckles vanish or having my hair curl. My guess is that I would have wasted my wish and asked for curls, never dreaming that the day would come when I could walk into a beauty parlor and come out with wavy hair.

Beauty wasn't the big thing with me, however; I wanted primarily to be a great actress and a brilliant writer. I couldn't decide which was preferable, so I settled for both. In exalted moments, of which I had an abundance, I was going to be a saint on the side.

Well, my freckles have disappeared and my hair is always more or less curly now; the other things are still just around the corner. I think I was about ten when my sister Juanita said something which made me realize that she wasn't planning to be a great celebrity in any field whatever; I was dumfounded.

"You mean you don't want to be *famous?*" I exclaimed.

I can still see the expression on her face; she looked as if she was smelling something offensive and touching a clammy object and hearing a raucous noise all at the same time.

"What *for?*" she asked.

An interesting question. I have never had any fame, but as near as I can judge from those who do, it is in much the same category as a pretty picture on your wall or a pair of becoming earrings, which are pleasant to have but don't do much for you in the pursuit of happiness. No, that's not quite accurate, because the painting and the earrings at least aren't disturbing, while almost all of the well-known people I have met seem more or less nervous for fear they will lose their prestige.

Having by now had quite a lot of time to think it over, the only art I would give a good deal to excel in is the art of living, although I suppose a person could become smug even about that if he was outstandingly good at it and conscious of great achievement. But this art does have two great advantages: unlike music, painting and the like, it is a field open to everyone and it doesn't require money or extra time. You don't have to pay for lessons, and you don't have to give up anything else in order to learn it and practice it. If you become really adept, you can hardly be narrow, exclusive, self-centered, and a bore, as any other artist, no matter how great, can well be without half trying. Also, everyone around you is benefited by your accomplishment.

Like any other art, however, the art of living takes some learning. Fortunately, we can do this learning on the job, so to speak, if we are willing to acknowledge mistakes and follow the few simple rules which come through when we listen to reason and common sense. Our lives are our own and the least we can do is blame nobody but ourselves if we make a mess of them.

Now let me ask you this: if you live your life to suit yourself, how can you possibly fail to make the most of it? Please don't jump to the conclusion that in order to do this you must be selfish and ruthless; it is one thing to refuse to take a friend to see a doctor because you had planned to go to a movie, but quite another to refuse to do many unnecessary things which you would prefer to skip. You probably don't feel that you would be acting selfishly if you saved your own money in order to see some plays or take a trip, so what is wrong in saving your own time for doing some reading? Whatever you do and whatever your circumstances, the point is to make the most of what you have and the best of what you cannot change.

I never went to college, but during the four years in which I might have gone, I had a variety of jobs, from nursemaid to telephone operator, which taught me a good deal, and a variety of experiences which taught me even more. In fact, I suspect that I learned more about life in those four years than a higher education could have taught me.

Of late, the emphasis on a college education has been extreme. For although it costs a lot of money, many a person spends four years memorizing a lot of things he isn't interested in, will no doubt make no use of nor ever enjoy, and certainly will forget. So why do they go? Except for those who are learning a profession, what do they expect to get out of it? I believe that many young people graduate without having been changed in any way that is going to make a particle of difference in their lives. And I would like to bet that those who do get something real and lasting out of their studies would have got something just as worthwhile out of those four years if they had spent them in another way.

One argument against that conclusion is that nowadays a person has trouble getting a job if he hasn't gone to college. Employers went overboard on this some years ago and at that time the young people I knew liked to say, "I've got to get a college education; I might want to apply for a job wrapping bundles at Macy's."

If your father should say to you, "Which do you want—to go through college or the eight thousand dollars it would cost?" it wouldn't be much of a risk to settle for the money; with it and with four years to look for a job you would be likely to find one.

It isn't easy to spot a college graduate by his point of view, by his fondness for reading, his value as a companion or his ability to express himself well or join in a conversation—or to know when not to join in. Not even by the grammar he uses nor by the job he holds. And whatever you do, don't be misled by the fanciful notion that college teaches you to think for yourself.

Travel, for those who enjoy it, is surely a worthwhile experience. I've done a little, but the truth is that although I enjoy traveling to some extent while I'm at it, it is only the little human incidents that stay with me: the sweet expression on an Italian woman's face while she helped me choose some fruit; the forlorn voice of the tourist in the American Express office when, getting no mail, he said, "I guess they've all forgotten me"; the rudeness of a taxi driver in Paris; the kindness of the Munich policemen; those sympathetic London bobbies; those amazing Russians who will take you in and feed you for a day, a month, or a year if you knock on their door and say you're hungry.

I have many such memories, but one doesn't have to travel over the world for such experiences; there are sad and rude and kind and helpful people everywhere. If that's the sort of thing that has meaning for you, you can get it in your own home town.

It wasn't until I was what you might call middle-aged that I was married. Then, after years of living in cities and being a "working woman," I was suddenly a wife. Fred and I moved to the country—Poverty Hollow, Redding Ridge, Connecticut—and I began a whole new career as cook, housekeeper, gardener. I've had a fair share of diversity, I suppose, for any one woman's life. But the important thing about a person is not what he or she has done, but what he or she *is*.

I am not an outstanding person physically, mentally, or spiritually. In our garden, I was able to dig an asparagus trench 240 feet long, two feet wide and two feet deep, not because I had a masculine physique but because I wanted a trench and knew that if I went about it sensibly, doing a little each day, I could swing it.

I haven't a brilliant mind but I make use of what there is of it, rather than be guided by what others may do, or say, or think. Spiritual? Well, I'm not the truly religious person that my Quaker mother was, but I think I have unconsciously adopted her unspoken attitude, which seemed to be that God didn't intend us to bother Him with every small detail; we are supposed to figure some things out for ourselves and act accordingly.

Like most people, I have had many ups and downs, and I have learned this: we can change or alleviate more of the downs than we would believe until we put our minds to it. And those we cannot change we can handle in some way far better than dwelling on them, either orally or silently. And don't imagine you are hiding worry and dissatisfaction just because you don't speak of them; they are written on your face.

Speaking of that face: the children are home from school, their father is due at any moment, so it is high time for you to put on some lipstick, powder your nose, and attend to your hair. As you glance in the mirror do you find that the eyes are restless, the muscles of the face somewhat tense, the whole effect one of strain? A clown paints various expressions on his face but you haven't learned that art; even the beauty parlor experts can't tell you how to do it.

No matter how shining your hair, how smooth your skin, how red your lips, the effect will still be less than appealing if your thoughts are negative. If you should mislay your brush and lipstick, try replacing them with a cheerful, relaxed frame of mind; your family and friends might appreciate the change.

Your thoughts are yours, to do with as you please, and how encouraging to know that the one thing in the world which you can control—your thinking—is the very thing you need to control in order to make headway in the art of living!

III

For Reluctant Cooks

MAN has made many changes on the earth, for better and for worse, but there's one thing which so far he hasn't outwitted: he still must eat if he wants to stay alive. Not only that, he likes to eat; whoever thought up that whole business did a comprehensive job of it.

Then, later, someone stumbled onto the idea of cooking and that, also, took hold in a big way. The result is that countless hours are spent each day preparing food; millions of women cook the year round, and for those who would like to skip it, all the cookbooks in the world calling it a joy aren't of much help.

There are, of course, women with a talent and love for the job; they grind and chop and mince and put through a sieve and cream and mix with this and that and stir and taste and add something, and stir and taste again. Are these women artistic perfectionists with cultivated palates or do they just love to cook? I don't know, but if cooking is their destiny, it's a fine piece of luck that they're so good at it and enjoy it.

But the many women who have to prepare meals every day without any special talent or liking for the job are in a bit of a fix. For almost any other work there's some element of choice; a girl who has to earn her living isn't compelled to choose, say, stenography. There are other types of work to try for which she may like better. And even keeping the house clean isn't as demanding as cooking, for to some extent you can do the cleaning at a chosen time, and even evade some of it now and then.

Cooking standards go up as we learn more about what is good for us. Not only should the food have a pleasant taste but also nowadays, when nutritionists are telling us what's what, we try to pay some attention to what they say, even though they change their minds occasionally. We are now told that vegetables should be cooked rapidly, should not be overcooked, and should be served the very minute they are done—another detail in the hectic job of getting everything ready at the same time and serving at once before the vitamins fly out the window.

As I go along I expect to include a few recipes, some because we think they're especially good, others because they're easy to prepare. I am leaving out the health angle almost completely because, for one thing, I'm not equipped to hold forth about it; for another, people don't much like to be told what's good for them. For myself, I don't feel happy about eating vegetables and fruits which have been sprayed with poison, or food that has been doctored in order to preserve it. I'm also disinclined to eat much of such things as white rice, flour, sugar, and other ingredients so refined that even weevils pass them up.

However, you will find some of these items in my recipes because that was the way I learned to make those particular dishes. Fred and I eat things that are "bad" for us so rarely, and we are both so healthy and so old, that they won't have a chance to do us any appreciable harm. But if I had children I would take the problem of feeding them most seriously, for I would be embarrassed if, twenty years from now, my daughter or my son, mumbling through dentures, were to say to me, "Didn't anyone *tell* you you were feeding us worthless junk, Mother?"

One way out of the dilemma of preparing endless meals is never to get into it: don't get married and have a family. Another way is to marry money, or make a lot yourself and hire a cook. I guess we can omit those good suggestions.

The most practical thing is not to try to evade the job but rather to put our minds to work to make it easier; this has many possibilities and angles. My first suggestion may seem too theoretical and vague to some of you, but I thoroughly believe in it, and the Bible supports me with, "As a man thinketh, so is he." Many cults and creeds have tried this out, seemingly to advantage, and psychologists and physicians have a good deal to say in its favor. Roughly, it is the belief that our thoughts and spoken words affect our bodies, minds, characters, and our likes and dislikes. My grandfather started me on this when he told me, that day, to look out of the right window.

I have heard a woman I know say often throughout forty years: "I *hate* to cook." She's actually a pleasant person, but when she says those words the expression on her face is far from attractive. If, during all that time, she had forced herself to think and to say aloud "I like to cook," or even "I don't mind getting dinner," my conviction is that by now she *wouldn't* mind it. If it had been impossible for her to say she enjoyed cooking, she could at least have tried never to think of her hatred; failing that, she certainly could have managed not to express it.

We might make a greater effort to improve our thinking if we had two photographs of ourselves hanging where we could look at them every day—one taken when we were dwelling on something pleasant and the other when thinking of something distasteful. We aren't pretty when we're hating, even if it's nothing more important than getting a meal, so that photograph might make us try harder to better our thinking.

What do we have, actually, except our thoughts, which we can call our own and can hold secure, no matter what goes on around us? Not our money, of course, which must be used for food, clothing, housing. Our material possessions can be lost or stolen or destroyed. Our hours are not our own; most of them belong to our families; some go to our friends; some, perhaps, to civic duties, or a cause; some are snatched out of our hands by unexpected demands.

But our thoughts are our very own. With practice and determination we can push Mrs. A. right out of our minds, if we don't like her, and think of Mrs. B., whom we love. If our husband was disagreeable at breakfast—well, maybe he slept badly. We can call to mind how thoughtful he was last Sunday, or, if absolutely necessary, go away back to the tone of his voice when he asked us to marry him. When we are washing a window we can think about how nice it will look when we've finished, instead of dwelling on the ones yet to be cleaned.

We can, if we try hard enough, search around and find someone else to blame for everything in our lives we don't like, except our thoughts. They can be protected if we have the strength of character to do it; we can blame no one but ourselves if our thinking is undesirable and makes us miserable. And if our thoughts are pleasant, what else matters?

Now to suggestions which may seem more practical, even if they aren't. Like many of us who are mediocre performers in the kitchen, you may have spurts of ambition; no doubt you have friends who are excellent cooks, and now and again you ask for some recipe, something your husband has eaten at their homes with obvious pleasure. If you get around to trying it, one of two things may happen: yours won't taste nearly as good as your friend's did, or you will think it's too much work. For you're handicapped; you have little talent or liking for the job, and the idea of spending maybe an hour or two preparing something which is eaten up so quickly seems silly to you. And tomorrow the dinner hour will strike again.

I was worse than a mediocre cook when I got married. This may have been because in a large family such as ours there was always someone who was better at it than I was and who liked to cook. Or maybe it was because for my mother life held many things more fascinating than food. But I suspect that the chief reason for my indifference was the fact that I read *Lorna Doone* when I was a little girl; Lorna was a delicate and fragile creature and the rough diamond who fell in love with her was bowled over by her aloof attitude to food. I probably decided to remain above coarse things such as caring what I ate.

I'm glad I can't remember how many years it took me to decide to reform. But within reason, of course; I knew that in order to excel in any field one had to really care, and no food I had ever eaten seemed worth the sacrifice of gardening or reading hours. So I labored and struggled until I became a good second-rate cook and, neither proud nor ashamed, let it go at that.

Then, a few years ago, when we went to the von Dumreichers' for dinner, Rosemarie served a leg of lamb which undermined my complacency. I didn't ask if it was much trouble or was difficult to prepare, because I had discovered that any talented cook's answer to such questions is No; to her it isn't. So I just asked for the recipe, which seemed to require a good deal more babying than I was accustomed to give a roast, but I was willing to tackle it.

Before I got around to it, we had Rosemarie and Franzi to dinner; they were to come early in the afternoon so that Franzi could dig up various bulbs and plants which we had promised him, and Rosemarie said she would teach me to prepare a veal stew. This was arranged on the telephone, Rosemarie checking up to see if I had everything she would need.

All went smoothly. Fred gave Franzi a hand outside so I was free to watch Rosemarie's every move. I have never eaten anything as good as that stew, and I wrote down the whole performance step by step, abandoning then and there my conviction that top-notch cooking required talent. Obviously all one had to do was carefully follow a good recipe.

A week or so later I tested that theory; I made another veal stew. It turned out to be much better than any I had ever made before, but it fared badly when compared to Rosemarie's. And I knew why.

It was true that I had watched Rosemarie's every movement; she would stir, taste, close her eyes, open them and gaze upward, then reach for the nutmeg, but the catch was that I didn't know exactly how much she had grated in. The next time she tasted she would reach again, but this time for another seasoning. I should have realized, then and there, that with the most perfect recipe in the world you wouldn't get very far if you didn't know which seasoning to reach for and how much to add. That sort of accomplishment one can comprehend, even if achieving it is beyond one's ability.

It's a fact, though, that Dottie Hoffman, another friend of ours, is an outstandingly good cook, and she doesn't measure and doesn't taste when she is preparing a dish. There's a conundrum for you.

I didn't give up immediately and neither did Rosemarie. She came over one afternoon and did a chicken with fresh tarragon, while I looked on and made notes. A week later I tried it; mine was good but the difference between the two was discouraging.

Then I realized I had been presumptuous. There are geniuses in cooking as in any other field; why should a person without any talent for this art presume to compete with them? Many of us (perhaps too many) want to write, and do, but unless we are overburdened with conceit, we don't aspire to rival Dostoevski. It's one thing to compose a little tune, another to be a Brahms.

If you have no gift for painting a picture or writing a melody you can skip these activities, but the majority of women are obliged to fix meals, however little they may like the idea. And for these countless women who have no special bent for cooking but who would like to do the job as acceptably (and painlessly) as possible, I don't believe the Rosemaries and the fine chefs would be the proper teachers.

I think run-of-the-mill cooks can learn more from a person in their own category, someone who has struggled with the same problems and faced the same handicaps that they have. My aim isn't (need I say?) to try to teach anyone how to become a wonderful cook and housekeeper, but I do hope I can pass on to you a few of the things I've learned which may make your job a little easier and pleasanter, and perhaps even make your meals taste a little better.

One evening Fred and I sat down to a dinner which was perhaps a little worse than usual, or else Fred wasn't very hungry and required something at least bordering on the palatable. Anyway, he took a bite or two of the main dish, then said, "I know when I'm licked."

So, as a matter of fact, did I, and we went to a restaurant.

At last, realizing that the food I had been expecting Fred and our guests (not counting me) to eat was too close to inedible, I began to study cookbooks. That must have been more than twenty years ago, and at first I meticulously followed rules and ingredients and measurements. When I finally began to substitute, or add, or subtract ingredients, according to my judgment or to what I had on hand, I was scarcely aware of it.

One day I was discussing with a friend some dish I had just made, and she said, "You're such an imaginative cook. I wouldn't dare treat a recipe with the disrespect you do."

I was surprised and assured her that I followed recipes conscientiously. She questioned this and asked me to look up the one under discussion. I had made this dish without the book for quite a while, and when I read the recipe aloud I was taken aback to discover that the only ingredient I hadn't exchanged for something I liked better was onions.

My young friend was exultant and, thinking that she was praising me, exclaimed, "I told you that you were creative."

When I "create" in cooking it is usually simply a matter of convenience. A young bride who lived near us used to run over and ask me how to make this and that, and one day she said laughingly, "Most of your recipes end the same way: '. . . or just use anything suitable you have in the icebox.'"

I constantly do that and I'm in favor of it—it can be both handy and economical—but one disadvantage is that if you should prepare something which turns out to be divine, you probably never will be able to duplicate it. Anyhow, a recipe is like anything else that has been conceived by the human mind; it's quite possible that it isn't perfect, and there's no reason why one shouldn't try to improve it. In many dealings with life we're helpless, but there's no law, moral or legal, which compels us to respect and obey a recipe if we don't choose to.

I've often observed that first-class cooks are hampered by ideas of perfection and are unlikely to settle for easy dishes. More than that, they rebel when I suggest a dish to them if the preparation is too simple. A friend of mine can't bring herself to serve her husband's favorite, creamed dried beef, for the main course at dinner, even when they're alone and even though she also likes it. Her artistic temperament rebels, and what can one do about that?

Neither can she bring herself to make a meal of navy (or pea or marrow) beans boiled with salt pork, although both she and her husband come back for at least a second helping when I serve them this really delicious dish.

BEANS WITH SALT PORK

(Or use split peas or lentils or dried limas.) A five-minute meal as far as labor is concerned.

Soak one package of beans overnight. The next morning add more water if the beans aren't generously covered with it. Peel a good-sized onion and put it in whole. Add a chunk of salt pork, either fat or lean, any size you like.

Just barely simmer this for several hours. Add salt and pepper to taste. If you are avoiding fat, cook the dish ahead of time, put in a cold place, and when the fat has congealed on top, take it off. Or skim the fat off when the dish is hot. When served, the beans should still be quite soupy; Fred likes them heaped on a slice of bread. With salad and dessert, this is for us a complete meal.

If you like raw onion, slices of sweet Spanish or Bermuda are a nice addition. And if you don't care for salt pork, use ham. Or put some frankfurters in the pot about five minutes before you are ready to eat.

A friend gave me a recipe which goes very well with this dish.

APPLE JELLY SAUCE

1 large glass apple jelly
2 teaspoons vinegar
½ teaspoon cloves
¼ teaspoon cinnamon
1 teaspoon dry mustard

Bring jelly and spices to a boil, then put into a pitcher and serve hot.

There's one strike against that sauce: it's one of those last-minute jobs which I avoid whenever feasible. That is, although you can put all of the ingredients into a pot ahead of time, you still have to heat it at the last minute. A trifle, yes, but our lives are cluttered with trifles. So I experimented; I made the sauce, poured it back into the empty glass and let it cool; now it was a highly-spiced jelly instead of a hot sauce and it tasted, we thought, just as good. The next step, of course, was to make several glasses at once to have ready to serve, and we've discovered that it's good with practically any kind of meat.

Lack of confidence can be a real hazard in cooking, as in other areas of life. Perhaps one of the reasons why so many otherwise excellent cooks can't come through with a first-class pie is that long ago the word got around that there's something tricky, even mysterious, about making a good crust. In my life I have known less than a dozen women who could make what I call a really delicious pie. They all knew *the* secret, the catch being that this varied; the fat must be cold and hard, one would say. Another, don't handle the dough. Use ice water. Use hot water. Put the dough in the refrigerator. One woman insisted it was the shape of her mixing bowl that spelled success for her.

I kept asking questions, kept trying. I was determined to learn how to make a pie that I myself could really enjoy and, brought up on Grandma Stout's pies, my standard was high.

Then someone gave me a Non-stick Pastry Kit, a basket-weave piece of material on which you roll out the dough, and a knitted cover for the rolling pin. This helped but it couldn't perform miracles.

One day I decided to use chicken fat for a pie crust, and it was close to wonderful. I tried this again a week later with very good results and I told a friend about it (like me, she usually made just fair pies, with now and then a winner); she said she had recently discovered that her best pies were made with bacon grease, although the bacon flavor wasn't an asset. After some strenuous thinking we hit on the thing that chicken fat and bacon grease have in common: they don't get really hard, as lard and vegetable fats do, and the moment you remove them from the refrigerator, they begin to get quite soft.

So we both experimented with lard, letting it get quite soft before using it, and at last our pies, if not remarkable, are always first-rate. Now we make them with some confidence.

There is a snag here, though; you can make a superior pie with soft fat but experts say (and I'm afraid that I must go along with them) that for a really flaky crust, hard fat is indispensable. I overcome this obstacle by going easy on the amount of soft fat I use; then, when I roll out the dough, I put dabs of hard, cold lard on it, fold it over, and roll again. This works very well.

As near as I can figure it out, the reason the soft fat does a better job is because you can incorporate it more thoroughly, one single bit after another, with the flour; this makes your dough stick together and easy to handle. Also, you need less water (or milk); I never use more than two tablespoonfuls to one cup of flour.

The main thing is to let your shortening get soft before using it; aside from this I have no suggestions about making a pie. All the cookbooks will explain exactly how to do it, but just don't let them talk you into thinking it's difficult, and forget all that ice-cold nonsense.

But what about those women who make top-notch pies with cold hard lard? Well, if in a long lifetime I had met hundreds of them, I wouldn't feel that I had discovered anything about shortening, but I've known so many good cooks whom pie crust defeats, so few who can produce an outstanding pie, that I'm forced to believe that those few are simply geniuses whom nothing daunts, not even hard lard.

I can't tell you much about pie fillings because I stick to five kinds. The only fruit pies I make are cherry, apple, and rhubarb. Many cookbooks, I believe, tell you to thicken the juiciest fruits a little, but we don't go for that. I put the fruit in the lower crust with the desired amount of sugar or honey and dot it generously with butter; add a dash of nutmeg and either vanilla or almond flavoring if you like. And cinnamon on apples if you care for it. Sometimes I add a few spoonfuls of sherry; as far as I know I originated this, although many cookbooks may recommend it.

To keep the juice from running over into the oven I moisten a strip of white cloth and put it all around the edge of the pie; I also put a pan a little larger than the one containing the pie; on the bottom shelf of the oven to catch any juice the cloth may not take care of. Anything rather than clean an oven.

I bake all pies at 500 degrees for ten minutes, then 450 for fifteen minutes, and 350 until done.

I believe pies have better flavor if you make them in advance and put them, unbaked, in the freezer; perhaps I think this only because I hate to do anything at the last minute. When you have guests for dinner it's very handy not to have to think up a dessert; just take a pie from the freezer and bake it.

The other two kinds of pie I make are pumpkin and sugar. For these I put only the shells into the freezer, although I do keep on hand a few containers with two cups of frozen pumpkin in each, ready to use for a pie. Any general cookbook will have a recipe for pumpkin pie filling.

As for sugar pie, I think Grandma Stout invented it. Whenever she had a little dough left over she would make a small one, but they became so popular with her nine grandchildren that she was wheedled into making more of them than any other kind. It's still my favorite, and with flourishing health and all my teeth and no weight problem, I have no qualms about eating it a few times a year.

SUGAR PIE

Line a pan with pie dough. For a nine-inch pie put one and a half cups of sugar and three fourths cup of flour on top of the dough and stir with your finger until they are well mixed. Be careful not to make a hole in the dough. Add one cup of milk and cream combined (as much cream as your diet permits) and stir again, gently but thoroughly, using a teaspoon. Now dot with butter, all the traffic will bear.

Grandma used only the above ingredients, but this is obviously a recipe you can do some fooling around with. Nutmeg? Almond flavoring? Brown sugar instead of white? Nuts? Cocoanut? I myself have never tampered with the original. Does one take paint and brush and presume to improve a Rembrandt?

IV

A Matter of Taste

When housekeeping and cooking became my fate, another activity accompanied it—gardening. Discovering at once that I liked growing things better than I liked cooking them, I began to figure out quick and easy ways to get food prepared and onto the table.

As I've told you, the time came when I realized that just getting the food cooked wasn't enough; it should also be palatable. Much later came Rosemarie with her high ideals in that field. And then we met Pierre. He could become so lyrical over, let us say, fresh fish with some superb sauce or other, that unwittingly he tricked me into believing that elaborate cooking might be a worthwhile aim.

But he made the mistake of lending me a la-de-da French cookbook which soon stifled my feeble ambition; almost every recipe was far too fancy for me to tackle. If I had a thousand years to live and needed only two hours of sleep out of the twenty-four, perhaps I would be willing to spend some of my valuable time chopping and grinding and stirring and straining and tasting. But life being short and me needing eight hours of sleep—well, I just couldn't work that sort of thing in.

Moreover, from my point of view there was perhaps an even better reason for my attitude toward that fancy cookbook. There were, for instance, a large number of chicken recipes, each one more involved than the last and all of them, if prepared properly, no doubt excellent. Pierre concocted one for us and it was divine. However, it tasted more of the sauce than of the meat, as I suspect most of the others would, and the fact is that it's quite all right with me if what I taste is just chicken when I eat it; I like the flavor. If you have a young fresh bird, can you do better by it than to broil or fry it? And later on in a fowl's life, how can a cook hope to improve on chicken and dumplings? Besides, it's so simple, requiring very little time and no talent at all.

In my opinion, most cooks don't do a good job of frying chicken, although it's an easy thing to do well. For almost any kind of frying an iron skillet is best, I think; I have two small ones which exactly fit the burners of my stove and that, too, is important.

FRIED CHICKEN

For this I prefer a young roasting fowl. You can rub the pieces with garlic if you like, then mix flour, salt, and pepper together, roll the pieces in this, and put them into a skillet with a generous amount of fat, heated just enough so that the chicken will barely sizzle when it is put in.

Brown the pieces slowly on one side, which should take about fifteen minutes. Then turn them. When all of them have been turned, put a cover on, but leave it a little to one side so that the chicken will fry rather than steam. Be sure to keep the fire low; the chicken should just barely sizzle at all times.

If you want gravy, remove the chicken when it's tender, pour off most of the grease, stir in some flour and as it cooks add very creamy milk gradually until you get the desired thickness. Salt and pepper to taste and a little sherry if you feel festive. Simmer gently. The whole performance takes about one hour.

Even if cooking isn't your talent, you can hold up your head and look any expert in the eye when you serve chicken and dumplings, for it's so easy to make it good. It's odd, but light, delicious dumplings are considered difficult to make; actually there's nothing easier. They can be mixed ahead of time and can cook while you have a second cocktail.

The only stumbling block in preparing this dish is finding an old eight- or nine-pound chicken. In these snappy days of quick turnover we hurry up and kill chickens before they have a chance to become the fine flavorful food they could be. As with turkey, beef, and pork, Fred and I think the older chickens have the best flavor; you have to cook them a long time and slowly, that's all. We used to get a suckling pig for Fred's birthday each year but we don't any more, not only because we think the older animals have a much better taste, but also the poor little pig looked like a new-born babe lying there in the refrigerator, and my nervous system couldn't take it.

My guess is that many shoppers buy the younger specimens only because they are likely to cost more and people think that therefore they must be better. This is a common attitude, and in cases where a person hasn't enough knowledge or experience to trust his own judgment, it's defensible. But it seems foolish to me not to at least try the cheaper kinds and find out for yourself whether or not they are satisfactory. I was told by a friend who worked in a factory which made a well-known brand of mayonnaise that the company puts up two varieties with different trade names and labels. One was priced considerably higher than the other, but the mayonnaise was identical; it all came out of the very same vat, or pot, or whatever they use. The expensive brand was for those who automatically buy "the best," the cheaper was for those who couldn't afford to pay the higher price. We can only hope that at least a few adventurous souls are bold enough to sample both kinds and are willing to trust their own taste. In a similar vein, a survey I read on canned peas said that uniformity in size was the big factor in the price—in other words, you pay extra for the satisfaction of having the peas you buy match each other. Somewhat on the order of matched pearls.

Old age *can* be a bit of a handicap in some things. Corn and asparagus, for instance, shouldn't be even a day too old for the best flavor and tenderness. But other vegetables, such as parsnips, kale, late cabbage, are supposed to be sweeter if they are exposed to some frosts. Tomatoes, for eating raw, must be allowed to ripen but, unlike corn, don't deteriorate if kept for some days after they are ready to eat. Peppers, in my opinion, are much better when ripe, although almost everyone eats them green and many people don't even know that they get bright red if left to ripen. Young carrots are good, of course, but I would like to line up a few dozen people who think they are so much more tender and sweeter than the big ones and feed them slices of each kind and see how many, if any, could tell the difference. If you grow them it's a good deal less work, for one thing, to let some of them get full size before you eat them. The point I am trying to make, however, is that some animals, some vegetables, and even some people, have a finer flavor when they are old.

But back to the chicken and dumplings I was going to tell you how to make with so little work.

THE CHICKEN

The fatter the fowl the better, for flavor, but a good deal of the fat should be skimmed off when the chicken is done.

Put the pieces in a large pot, add a whole onion, some garlic if you like it, salt and pepper, and about two cups of sherry. Simmer this very gently, with the thicker pieces on the bottom. If the wings and such get done sooner than the rest, I remove them from the pot.

When the chicken is tender, put it onto a platter and into a warm oven. Then skim the fat off the liquid. You will find that you haven't enough liquid for dumplings. The reason you shouldn't start with more is because it would have got all of the flavor; the liquid would be good but the meat flat.

THE DUMPLINGS

Sift two level cups of flour with four level teaspoons of baking powder and one level teaspoon of salt. Add six tablespoons of fat (lard or pork drippings or bacon grease are best) and mix with pastry mixer. Now add one cup of milk, then mix thoroughly and hard with a spoon.

Now add water to the liquid in the pot until you have altogether eight cups or more. This added water has made the soup flat, so you put in a package or two of dehydrated chicken soup. (Don't use canned soup). Season to taste, bring to a boil, then slowly drop in the dough in small portions. The water should not stop boiling. Cover tightly and simmer fifteen minutes.

OR BISCUITS

If you should want to make biscuits with this dough, instead of dumplings, grease pans lightly, drop chunks of dough, not touching each other, onto the pans. Bake in 400-degree oven until done.

I'm not keen on sauces, but just to show you how broad-minded I am, I'll now give you a recipe for veal with sauce. I got it from the French cookbook Pierre lent me, and although Fred and I are both extremely fond of breaded veal cutlet, we find this dish a welcome change. For this, one may use a fryer in which the meat sticks to the pan because, for once, that fault is an advantage; it seems to improve the sauce.

VEAL CUTLETS OR CHOPS WITH MUSTARD SAUCE

Brown the cutlets, or chops, rather slowly in a lightly greased skillet, turn the meat, and cook until done. Put on hot platter and keep warm in oven.

In a pan blend two tablespoons vinegar, one generous teaspoon French mustard, one teaspoon butter, three tablespoons cream, two teaspoons olive oil, salt, and pepper. Stirring, heat this but don't let it boil. Now put it in the pan from which you have removed the meat, scrape off into the sauce the brown juices which are stuck to the pan, and heat again, but don't let the sauce come to a boil at any time—that is important. Pour over the veal and serve, or serve separately. Some people may prefer the meat without the sauce.

One of my sisters discovered that when she warmed up a left-over piece of the veal in sauce, it tasted better than when first cooked. This is fine, for it means it's a dish you can make in advance and then just put in a low oven and heat.

Now, how would you like to have a roast (beef, pork, veal, lamb, turkey, goose, chicken—you name it) which keeps you in the kitchen for a total of ten minutes at the very most? Here's the secret:

I think it was in 1950 that a friend gave me a copy of Adelle Davis's book *Let's Cook It Right.* It was most helpful, but what really fascinated me were a few paragraphs headed "Slow Roasting." The idea appealed to me but the directions weren't very specific, so I wrote and asked Miss Davis a few questions. We became friendly by mail and on her next trip East (she lives in California) we had her here for cocktails. I asked her, "Why on earth didn't you give more details about slow roasting in your book?" and she replied, "Because I had no hope that anyone would try it; the idea is too new and different."

An interesting observation and she was probably right. For

it seems that most women don't mind adopting a new hair-do, even though it may make them look fairly ridiculous, provided others are adopting the same thing; this makes it "in style." But inertia, conservatism, timidity, fear of ridicule seem to block many of us if it's a matter of doing, all alone, something different and new. Maybe this is as it should be, but I doubt it.

I find the slow-roasting method of cooking meat superior to the usual method, but before I tried it we had to pay twenty-five dollars to have a new thermostat, which begins to register at 150 degrees, put on our stove. (Our old one began at 250.) This may sound like a reckless procedure, since the venture was as yet untried, but when I'm sold on an idea I'm really gone, and Fred went along with me. We also had to buy a meat thermometer.

The first thing I attempted to slow-roast was rare roast beef. My niece Virginia and my sister Mary were visiting us for a few days, and shortly before dinnertime one evening, Virginia and I rubbed a piece of beef with pork drippings and carefully inserted the thermometer. I was putting the meat into a pan when Mary, who hadn't yet heard about the new idea for roasting, came into the kitchen. Knowing we were having chops that night, she glanced at the beef and said: "What's that?"

"It's the meat for tomorrow night," I replied. "I'm going to put it in the oven."

"*Now?*" she exclaimed.

"Certainly, who doesn't?" put in Virginia blithely.

Following instructions, we started it at 250; after an hour I turned the thermostat as low as possible—150. Rare roast beef is done when the meat thermometer reaches 135 to 140 degrees. I couldn't set the thermostat as low as that, but Miss Davis had said to roast the meat twenty-four hours and I thought she must know that 150 degrees was the lowest one could get on a thermostat. I felt relatively safe.

Of course I looked at the meat thermometer the first thing the next morning; it hadn't reached 130 degrees. All day long I kept checking, and toward dinnertime it still hadn't reached 135, so I set the thermostat slightly higher. By seven o'clock the meat thermometer read 138.

Virginia and Mary hovered near as I took the meat out of the oven. The outside was black. My heart sank.

"Is it all right?" they asked, simultaneously and sympathetically. (And maybe, too, they were hungry.)

"Search me," I replied, trying to sound as if it didn't matter much either way.

I took the platter of meat to the table, set it down, and proceeded to cut a slice from the burned-looking chunk. And revealed a miracle: lovely, rare meat, juicy and tender. In other words, it had worked.

Slow roasting is equally successful with any other kind of meat. A fowl, roasted twenty-four hours, can be carved with your fingers; that is, the legs and wings simply fall off if you take hold of their tips and gently pull. Yet the meat isn't overdone; the low heat keeps it from over-cooking. The slow roasting holds in all the juices, there is no shrinkage, and the stuffing is full of chicken flavor. Another advantage is that you can use an old, inexpensive chicken and it will be completely tender. But the skin will be hard unless, as a friend of ours, Gordon Page, suggested, you seal the whole chicken with aluminum foil. This, or a brown paper bag, works perfectly and I now wrap all roasts with one or the other.

If you try this slow method, be very sure to put your thermostat at 250 for the first hour; I once failed to do this, with the result that the meat had a terrible taste, as if it had spoiled. Also, be sure not to leave the thermostat at 250 overnight; your meat would over-cook.

Adelle Davis says that fewer vitamins are lost if meat is always cooked slowly, whether on top of the stove or in the oven. She also says less electricity is used in slow-roasting than in the usual method and I think this must be true, because the indicator is almost always off at that low heat. Also on the plus side is the fact that the oven never gets greasy. Another great boon is that if your oven is set at the temperature which you want the meat to be when done (and this is possible for everything except rare roast beef), it cannot over-cook. Let's say you expect to serve dinner—a roast—at seven, but your guests are delayed an hour. The meat will be just as good at eight as it would have been at seven.

In doing a large pork roast which is ready when the meat thermometer reaches 165, you will find you have to set your oven a little higher than 165. With a veal or lamb roast and with chicken and turkey, I've discovered that the meat is done before the meat thermometer has quite reached the required number of degrees, so I serve it. Of course, I wouldn't take a chance on pork. As a matter of fact, the first few times you try this slow method you should begin to watch the meat thermometer a few hours before dinnertime, moving the thermostat up or down according to how the meat is progressing. But you will soon get onto the various tricks, and the time will come when you have to check only once or twice.

In Adelle Davis's book she gives some information about the different grades of meat (particularly beef) which I would be willing to bet would astonish the great majority of housewives. There are seven official United States grades of beef: prime, choice, good, commercial, utility, cutter, and canner. Miss Davis tells us that: "All government-inspected meats, regardless of grade, are examined for disease and are handled with equal care under the same sanitary conditions." So we don't have to shrink from the cheaper grades on that score. The essential point, as she says, is that the lower grades are thus labeled not because of inferior quality or flavor but merely because of the age of the animal and therefore its degree of toughness. If properly cooked there's nothing against them. On the contrary, Miss Davis finds the flavor of these meats superior and fervently recommends them.

Well, I put two and two together (Miss Davis's information and her slow-roasting idea) and sure enough, I came up with the right answer: one could oven-roast old tough beef satisfactorily. But don't think we didn't have difficulty trying to find a commercial grade. The butcher would look at us with indignation and suspicion; were we planning to report him for passing off cheap grades of meat for expensive ones? Were we suggesting that he would handle anything as disreputable as fourth-grade meat? He didn't actually ask these questions but we sensed them in his manner and actions, and the more pained he looked, the more we suspected that perhaps he *was* a little shady in his policies.

We found we weren't going to be able to get any commercial beef by buying just a few pounds at a time, so we asked our regular butcher if he would get us a forequarter of the commercial grade. He said he would, then asked, "How did you get on to that beef? We call it Butchers' Choice; it has much better flavor than the high-priced grades, only most women don't know how to cook it to make it tender."

I told him about slow-roasting and he was most interested. Here, to round up the details, is what you do.

SLOW ROASTING

For everything but pork and a leg of lamb, rub the roast thoroughly with fat; pork drippings are very good for this. Don't salt the meat; that's supposed to draw out the juices, but pepper it and rub garlic over it if you wish.

Insert the thermometer into the thickest part of the roast, being careful to avoid bone and fat. Put in a cold oven, with the thermostat at 250 degrees, and turn the oven on to "bake." After one hour adjust the thermostat to whatever heat the meat should reach when done. (You will find this information on your meat thermometer.)

The meat may be put in the oven anywhere between twenty-four and thirty-six hours before you expect to serve it. If it's lamb, for instance, the thermostat, after the first hour at 250, is set at 185. If you're planning to serve dinner at seven, and at three P.M. *the meat thermometer has reached 185, the lamb is done but it can't overcook if the thermostat is set at 185. On the other hand, if you check about an hour before you want to serve the meat and find the thermometer is at only 160, you will have to give the oven more heat. After you have done a few roasts you will find it's extremely simple to adjust your thermostat to prevailing conditions.*

One of the most important things is to be sure to adjust the thermostat after that first hour at 250 degrees. Just last evening, after dinner, I put a roast into the oven, set the thermostat at 250, set the timer to ring in an hour and went into the living room, closing the door behind me. I settled on the couch with a book and Fred began playing some records. Beethoven went *fortissimo* at the wrong moment for me; I didn't hear the timer and completely forgot the meat in the oven. Luckily, as I started to bed two hours later I smelled something good and remembered the roast.

There are other ways of cooking meat which, as far as time required just before dinner is concerned, are as easy as roast. Haven't you heard a business woman say, wistfully, that she and her husband are very fond of stews and pot roast but can rarely have them? It's easy, though. She could buy enough stewing meat for two or three meals, and some evening when she's going to be in the kitchen for a while doing something else she could also brown this meat, which takes only a few minutes, and put it on to simmer until bedtime. The next evening when she gets home from work she could put some frozen carrots and canned potatoes in the pot and have a good stew. A pot roast could be handled the same way.

And here's a dish which is easy on the producer and seems to be a favorite with consumers.

BEEF WITH DUMPLINGS

Brown stew meat (enough for at least two or three meals) at some time when you have to be in the kitchen anyway. Store it in meal-sized containers in the freezing compartment. If you are having guests later that week, some evening beforehand simmer some of the browned meat with a cup or two of water added; put in refrigerator before you go to bed.

The evening that your company is coming, put the meat on the simmerer again as soon as you get home from work. Add enough water to cover generously, and a bouillon cube for each cup of water. When the meat gets hot, taste, then season (perhaps more bouillon, salt, pepper, a little curry) until it has enough flavor to share with the dumplings, which you make (see "Chicken and Dumplings") and put into the pot fifteen minutes before you want to eat.

I'm not a gravy expert but I've learned a trick or two. It was our friend Gordon Page again who gave me this idea: if you want gravy with a roast, you don't have to fuss around and make it just before the meal. Stay a jump ahead of the game by having at least one container of gravy in the freezing compartment and use that with tonight's roast. Then, later, make another batch with tonight's meat juices and put it into the freezer for the next time.

Fred prefers thin gravy because it soaks into the bread instead of running around in his plate, and I prefer it because the flavor is intact and also it's less trouble. But thin gravy won't sink into potatoes, so the thing to do is to persuade your family artfully that bread is better with it than potatoes. Then you not only don't have to thicken the gravy, but you also don't have to cook potatoes. Two birds, if I ever saw them.

I'm going to give you the recipe for veal stew which Rosemarie gave me. As I told you, mine wasn't nearly as good as hers; a perfect recipe doesn't make a culinary artist out of you, or at least it doesn't out of me. But you may be a better cook than I am.

VEAL STEW À LA ROSEMARIE

Veal for stewing
A few onions
Mushrooms, canned or fresh
Salt
Pepper
Paprika
Bouillon cubes
Sour cream
Nutmeg
Worcestershire sauce
Flour

Sauté onions, mushrooms, paprika. Then flour, salt, and pepper the veal and sauté it separately, until water rendered by meat is almost evaporated. Add the onion mixture and a bouillon cube in water to the meat and let simmer gently. One half hour before serving add sour cream, nutmeg, dash of Worcestershire sauce. If too liquid add moistened flour. Stir often but gently. Serve with rice, if you wish.

If you bake a half or a whole ham (any cookbook will tell you how), you can keep it for two or three weeks in the refrigerator. You could serve it for dinner a few times; cut off thick generous slices and heat in the oven. That apple jelly which I spoke of, either hot or cold, is especially good with it. Ham is popular for Sunday breakfast, and nice for a sandwich for Sunday supper. I hope you will buy a ham with a bone in it and use the bone to make a split pea dinner.

Of late years casserole meals have become popular, but I can't understand why women who know and care more about food than I do so often serve flat-tasting casseroles. I think that one trouble is that good cooks have such lofty aspirations; they're glad to settle for a one-dish meal but it must be different and fancy. Heaven forbid that it merely be good to eat.

For the baked casserole which contains both meat and

starch, I think you must use either pork, or chicken with bacon, for your meat. Ham might do, but I think pork is better. If you want to use other meats, pork should be added also.

A dozen or more years ago Fred gave me a cookbook of just casserole recipes—180 of them. You may find it hard to believe but, fan though I am of this easy dish, I have adopted only three of these, and I have distorted even them until the originator would never recognize them.

Now I am not claiming that I have tried the entire 180 and found them wanting, but I *have* given a few dozen of them a trial, and have read every one. Some are just too fancy, others call for ingredients I never have, such as red perch and pigeon, of all things! Still others are too simple (such as egg affairs which Fred looks down on for the main course at dinner), and some of them don't sound attractive enough to try even once.

The two chief advantages of a casserole are that you can prepare it ahead of time and your meat and starch can be in one dish. A frozen vegetable (or a fresh one, washed and in the refrigerator) will cook in ten minutes and, with dessert prepared in advance, dinner is served.

Here is one of my casserole recipes.

PORK, BEEF, AND VEAL WITH RICE

About ½ pound each of beef and veal, about 1 pound pork in chunks
3 onions
A can or two of mushrooms (or fresh ones)

1¼ cups of raw brown rice
3 or 4 bouillon cubes or 3 cans consommé
Salt and pepper

Sauté onions, add meat and mushrooms. In greased casserole put rice, add meat mixture, salt, and pepper. Dissolve the bouillon cubes in three cups of hot water and pour over the whole mixture. Cover and put in oven at 350 degrees for one and a half hours or until done.

You can skip either the beef or veal or substitute chicken for either. I wouldn't want to leave out the pork but I would, reluctantly, substitute ham for it.

The preparation of this dish takes only about fifteen minutes and it's popular with our friends; even those who are reducing can't resist a second helping.

This is another popular one.

SPAGHETTI AND CHICKEN

1 pound or more left-over chicken (or canned chicken)
1½ 8-oz. packages spaghetti
1 large can tomatoes
1 can mushrooms
3 medium-sized onions
1 green pepper (you can skip this)
A few bacon slices
Salt and pepper

Let's start with cooking the spaghetti. Italians (the masters of spaghetti cooking, I guess) and tradition tell you to cook the macaroni-spaghetti family in lots of boiling water. I prefer the following:

Bring to a rolling boil one and a half cups of water and add, so slowly that boiling doesn't stop, one and a half cups of spaghetti and pepper and salt. Cover the pot and simmer until tender. The only objection to this method is that it isn't very easy to measure spaghetti by the cupful. I get around this by breaking it up into a glass pitcher which has cups marked on it. (I find this pitcher handy for many things.)

While spaghetti is cooking, fry the bacon (I cut mine up a little first), remove it from the skillet, and sauté pepper and onion until golden. Add chicken, tomatoes, mushrooms (drain juice off and save).

Grease a casserole dish, and starting with the spaghetti put it and the chicken mixture into the dish in layers. Pour the tomato and mushroom juice over the whole mixture, sprinkle with grated cheese. Bake at 350 degrees for about thirty-five minutes.

You can use pork instead of chicken. Ham would be good, too.

I'm not brave enough to serve fish to guests, but Fred and I like this salmon casserole very much.

SALMON IN WINE AND EGG SAUCE

1 can salmon (or fresh, if you prefer)
Fresh uncooked peas or frozen ones
2 or 3 eggs
Cream sauce
½ cup white wine or sherry
¼ teaspoon basil
Salt and pepper

Hardboil the eggs. Make sauce, using the wine for part of the liquid. Chop or slice eggs and add to sauce. Put salmon in greased casserole, add uncooked peas, and pour sauce over all. Bake at 350 degrees for thirty minutes.

You can use either fresh or frozen peas or omit them and serve a vegetable separately. Or salad. You can also put some small potatoes into the salmon mixture, and there's your entire meal.

If you like the idea of casseroles, you may feel that only three recipes seems confining. Well, I never make these dishes (except the fish one) for just Fred and me, so we don't have them often enough to get tired of them. Anyhow, there's nothing to prevent you from making up some of your own. And you business women may like to double the recipe and store the surplus in the ice-chamber. The day you are going to have it for dinner, be sure to take it out before you leave for work, and all you will have to do when you get home is add a small amount of liquid (try a little sherry) and heat in the oven. A little grated cheese, too, will help.

Here is a valuable hint which someone told me: for any dish which calls for a sprinkling of bread crumbs on top, substitute prepared stuffing; this is crisp and has some flavor besides.

Now if we keep in our minds, or in a notebook, a list of quick, easy dishes for the days when we would rather be almost anywhere than in the kitchen, and another list of tastier but more troublesome meals for those times when we feel like paying the price, we are well-equipped for both moods. The fine thing about it is that we do have a choice.

To sum up my advice to reluctant and mediocre cooks, the main thing is to be courageous. Fear, we are told, is a help on those occasions when it's necessary to run for your life, but that happens rarely nowadays. All other fears—of sickness, old age, poverty, of other people's opinions, of change—merely handicap us. So follow your inclinations insofar as possible. Don't spend endless hours in the kitchen if you don't want to. Don't be afraid to add to or subtract from recipes, or to make up new dishes and, above all, don't let anyone shame you out of serving simple, easy meals if they taste good.

Don't forget that the main purpose of eating is to stay alive and healthy. Next comes enjoyment of the food, for which we need, primarily, just one thing: good flavor. Other things help: the crispness and the temperature of some foods make a difference; attractive color combinations are pleasant; variety doesn't do any harm. Sloppiness is an excellent thing to avoid. But if the food you serve tastes good, I doubt that anyone will mind that it took you only five minutes instead of five hours to prepare. Let others climb Mount Everest if they wish; you don't have to do it, thank goodness, just because it's there.

V

Guests—Welcome and Otherwise

SOME people are coming to dinner. Did you ask them for pleasure or was it an obligation? How are you going to proceed—give them a meal without a lot of fuss, or prove to them that you know what's what and can put on a show equal to anybody's? As near as I can remember, women used to entertain their friends and acquaintances primarily because they wanted to see them. Today, "paying back" seems to be the keynote. Some women I know wait until they "owe" a dozen or so people, then have them all at once, to "get it over with." Some say they invite certain couples together, so the lively ones will take the curse off the bores; others claim that it's better to have all the dull ones at one throw, suffering only once instead of several times.

A few seem to enjoy making a performance of a dinner party, and they gain a certain reputation; then they're stuck with it, even after they would like to let down. Some women have party-loving husbands who close their eyes to the work involved because they are kind-hearted and don't want to believe that someone else is paying for their fun. I know two women, both over middle age, who have entertained lavishly ever since they were married; both are equipped with kind hearts and considerate husbands—the women can't bear to admit that they've been fed up for a long time, and the men would hardly be able to stand it if they knew the truth.

Why do *you* invite people to your home? To please your husband or for your own pleasure or to pay back or to show off? If entertaining is often a headache, how can you either avoid it or make the best of it?

Your own temperament and circumstances must be taken into account. Perhaps you have the courage to drop most of the people whom you don't enjoy. And don't worry too much about this, for it could be that they have been dying to drop you. If you have a too-sociable husband, perhaps you can get him to compromise. If you like showing off, make very sure you aren't paying too high a price for the benefits you reap.

In other words, give the matter a dose of straight thinking. You can't always, perhaps, look forward to your guests with unadulterated joy, but surely there's something wrong with one's way of life if the very thing which is supposed to give pleasure is often actually a burden or a bore.

Some of the difficulty for those who find entertaining a wearisome problem comes, I suspect, from all this nonsense called "gracious living." If you are old-fashioned enough to think that a gracious hostess is one who is thoughtful, pleasant, relaxed, rather than one who serves a certain brand of coffee or wine and whose table is covered with fine linen, then you're on my side. It's true that if by waving a wand I could sit down to a magnificently appointed table, I wouldn't hesitate to wave enthusiastically three times a day. But standing over an ironing board, polishing candlesticks and supplying all the other fancy touches is too much for me to pay for such a pleasure. Beauty, like a trip abroad, may be an extremely desirable thing, but unless we happen to be rich in time, energy and money we are going to ask "How much will it cost?" before we plunge. And many hostesses may not have stopped to realize that if their table settings were a little less attractive their faces might be more so. In any case, I would like to give some backing to any woman who would like to stop going through fancy motions when she entertains, doing it not because her heart is in it but only because her friends do.

Many people dine simply when there is just the family, but put on a show for guests. No, that's an unfair and critical way to put it; rather, let us say that when they have guests they feel more festive if they doll things up a bit. That's fine, if they enjoy it, but as a rule I think it tends to make the housewife feel that entertaining is a big job, with the result that she keeps postponing it. Am I not right in saying that if you keep putting something off, it surely means you aren't eager to do it?

Year in, year out, I cook many meals for guests, and if I were to put on a performance each time I would be a crankier and tireder person than I already am. Not only that; I'm sure that if I had a reputation for elegance but practiced it only at dinnertime, I would be nervous through breakfast and lunch for fear someone would pop in and catch me living crudely.

If I seem to have labored this point it's because I have a strong feeling about it; I am furious with the advertisers for spoiling one of my favorite expressions. I have always felt that a gracious lady was about the best that anyone could ask for in ladies. The new conception is, of course, much easier for a person to achieve than mine; it is less difficult to have gleaming silver than a glowing spirit, so the country is getting cluttered with gracious ladies. I'll have to think up another expression for the kind I mean.

The advertisers incidentally have also played havoc with many other useful words. A man of distinction is no longer one who has actually distinguished himself; he has become a man who likes one brand of something better than another, and he has also become a joke. I have a neighbor who likes Salad Bowl lettuce better than Oak Leaf, while I prefer the latter; unfortunately, so far we haven't been able to figure out which one of us is therefore a woman of distinction and which one is merely a woman. An olive has become mammoth or colossal and, in a way, that's a break; it isn't always easy to define words for your children, so if you're asked the meaning of those two adjectives, just get out the olives.

But now people are expected for dinner, and whatever else you decide on I suppose you'll have cocktails with canapés. These latter can be awfully good without costing much in time or money. I have found that a practical way to choose the recipes you want to keep in your repertoire is to try them out on friends. One of mine is so universally and highly popular that it almost causes the dinner to go begging, and here it is.

CHOPPED EGG CANAPÉS

Hardboiled eggs
Spiced salt
Pepper
Garlic
Dehydrated onion
Sour cream
Mayonnaise
French mustard
Horseradish

Cut up or chop the eggs. Add everything else to taste. Skip the mustard if you have only that well-known brand which the radio announcers get so lyrical about, but by all means use a little French or German variety if you have it. You can also skip the garlic juice, but if you do use it I hope you have a garlic squeezer and will use a clove in making the juice, rather than garlic salt or powder. (Incidentally garlic keeps fresh almost indefinitely in a closed jar in the refrigerator, and so does horseradish.)

I find dried onion superior to the fresh for some purposes; it's quick and easy to use, and safe for people who can't digest raw onion. But shop around until you get a really good brand; I find onion powder *worthless.*

You can use only sour cream or only mayonnaise; I use both, about three times as much cream as mayonnaise.

Many of you must have tried anchovies and cream cheese, or cottage cheese. And left-over meat, particularly pork, ham, bacon, or chicken, chopped and mixed with sour cream or mayonnaise, makes good canapés; add hard-boiled egg if you need more bulk.

The drinks are Fred's department, and he has a slick way of making them in advance; when our guests arrive all he has to do is pour. He mixes up eight gallons each of Daiquiris and Manhattans and two of whiskey sours, using artificial lemon, because the fresh juice would spoil. Instead of sugar he uses honey, or a sugar substitute which isn't fattening. He keeps the cocktails in gallon jars but always has a half gallon of each kind in the refrigerator, thus eliminating any bother with ice cubes before serving.

Born in prohibition Kansas, I'll never forget the shock I got when, visiting in Chicago at the age of sixteen, I first saw an open saloon; I'm hardly exaggerating when I say that a shop displaying a sign "Murder at Reduced Rates" would have appalled me only slightly more. I myself was an abstainer through the frenzy of the twenties. However, I was broad-minded and went to parties where, by midnight, I was likely to be the only sober person present. Why I went I can't imagine; to a non-drinker a crowd of people under the influence has little appeal. I seem to remember that I signed the pledge once or twice, but I never was what you could call a teetotaller. In fact, I was so obliging that I would try just about anything, but one sip was always enough.

When Fred and I moved to the country, the things to do around the place were so fascinating that we had to think up some device to make us stop working and take a little rest before dinnertime. Fred came up with The Cocktail Hour and, not being an enthusiastic drinker of alcohol, he had sherry while I settled for tomato juice. Before long he graduated to something stronger and I became a sophisticated drinker who could down sherry, port, or dubonnet with a degree of pleasure.

Many doctors today agree that we should drink a certain amount of alcohol daily after we reach the age of forty; it has something to do with keeping the arteries from hardening. They may change their minds tomorrow about this, as authorities have a tendency to do, but meanwhile I suppose you can take a drink with the feeling that you're prolonging your life—provided, that is, you have faith in doctors' statements. And I don't know about you, but alcohol makes me feel tolerant. I may be annoyed at somebody, but after a few sips I find myself thinking, "oh, what the hell! I suppose he *means* all right, the dimwit." By the time my glass is empty I can even tolerate the idea of going to the kitchen and getting the evening meal.

One bad thing about drinking is the cost. It's easy to think up a relatively inexpensive but acceptable meal, but I know no way of serving economical drinks. Yet there's a seemingly prevalent idea that any gathering has to be started off with a round of drinks in order to get the ball rolling; even young people apparently have so little verve that they must have a stimulant before they can get going. As for old, tired people, I can see how this, alas, might be the case, but if they're that old and that tired, wouldn't they be better off if they stayed at home and went to bed?

Then there's the business of drinking to excess. How much is "excess"? Well, for one thing, it's the point at which it's detrimental to your health. As for the person who drinks so much that he feels miserable the next day, he has surely overdone it. And anyone at a party who drinks until he becomes either a bore or a nuisance has in my opinion had too much. Nothing done to excess is good, I suppose. However, you can over-eat and suffer alone, but the person who over-drinks is likely to victimize everyone around.

Still, with all its drawbacks, I love cocktail time, particularly if I'm the hostess. Instead of having to hurry off to the kitchen when the company arrives, I manage to have things arranged so that I, too, can relax for a while over the canapés and drinks. Actually it would suit me just as well if my drink was tomato juice; to me it isn't the liquor that's important, it's the somewhat tranquil interlude before the more involved affair of dinner.

Eventually, of course, to the kitchen I must go, but not to work very hard or very long.

Although in general I'm against serving soup to guests, I may start the meal in summer with

VICHYSSOISE

2 medium-sized onions	Sweet or sour cream
4 medium-sized potatoes	Chopped chives
2 tablespoons butter	Nutmeg
2 tablespoons flour	Salt
2 quarts chicken broth	

Sauté onions in butter until slightly brown. Add flour but do not brown it. Add peeled potatoes and broth and cook until potatoes are very soft. Force through sieve and cool to room temperature.

Green onions or leeks may be used for half the onion quota. Make the chicken broth from dehydrated chicken soup.

To serve, put into individual cups or bowls, drop in a good big blob of sour cream and sprinkle with chives and nutmeg.

This is very good and I beg you to try sour cream rather than sweet, even if you think you don't like sour cream.

If we're having a roast, for the starch I often serve small potatoes browned in a skillet, an easy, last-minute trick. One or two brands of canned cooked potatoes are about as good as fresh ones, and they don't cost much. Sometimes I boil very small ones with the jackets on about an hour before dinner, peel them and put them back in the pot and set the pot on the same electric burner, which is turned off but still hot. It takes only a few minutes after cocktails to heat a skillet, put in some fat (try soybean oil for this) and brown the potatoes in it. They're well-liked, too.

In August and September we often have corn-on-the-cob for the starch; nearly everyone is crazy about it, and since I steam it (for five minutes), the time it would take to get a pot of water boiling is eliminated. I pick it just before I cook it, and of course one of the guests always wants to go to the patch with me to "help."

With almost any meat except a roast, the starch is taken care of: rice or noodles in a casserole, dumplings with a stew or with chicken. As for steaks and chops for guests, thumbs down; that's a last-minute performance which I avoid.

If you care to, you can save money for the main course by eliminating some of the frills. Many a time I have seen women who have to watch their dimes, if not their pennies, serve, say, olives, celery, and salad on the same occasion, plus perhaps an expensive bit of cheese and other fancy small items. This is fine if you can afford it, or even if you can't but want to do it because of the festive feeling it gives you. But if you do it only because you're afraid of being criticized—well, if the worst thing people can think up to say about you is that you don't serve extras at a company dinner, you're lucky; I hope my friends can't think of anything more reprehensible to say about me when they're utilizing my share of their gossip time.

In the winter I let our guests choose the vegetables they prefer from the freezer. In summer, we're likely to have what's available in the garden. Then they are picked, washed, dried and put in the refrigerator in the afternoon (some nutritionists say that if a fruit or vegetable is to be cut up, you lose fewer vitamins if you chill it first).

Perhaps we're having a salad; the lettuce, spinach, dill, and parsley from the garden have been washed, then dried by putting them in a bag (mine was made by sewing two large dishrags together) which I swing briskly out in the yard. If you live in a city apartment, maybe you could swing the bag out of a window or over the bathtub. The point is that the greens should be thoroughly dried before they are put into the refrigerator and this is an effective way to do it. A few minutes before dinner the salad ingredients are broken into small pieces and put into a large wooden bowl. A German writer we know, who is so highbrow that I understand very little he says, did make it clear to me that the first step in making a salad should be: put the oil on and toss until the greens are well coated with it; it keeps them from wilting. I use soybean oil, and half as much vinegar as oil. Wine vinegar is wonderful for salad; I use either that or cider vinegar, according to how rich I feel at the moment. I squeeze a clove of garlic over the greens, then add dried onion, spiced salt, and pepper. I taste before adding any regular salt since the spiced kind is usually sufficient. For the tossing I may call on a guest, who then puts the salad into the individual cherrywood bowls which Fred made. The best salads I've ever eaten were served in Chinese restaurants; mine aren't *that* good, but people do seem to enjoy them, and I give the credit to the fresh dill and to the superior seasonings.

Now what about dessert? We are told by doctors that nearly everyone eats too much, so as a rule I'd vote for something simple and sensible after a hearty meal. Jello, berries (fresh or frozen), sliced peaches or some other fruit. But perhaps your family or friends or you yourself have a hankering for richer and grander desserts, and for these I have a few suggestions.

If you want to serve strawberry shortcake and will use the biscuit dough recipe in this book, I think you will like the result. I make the biscuits rather large, and bake them while we're having dinner. Then I open them with a sharply pointed knife, quickly butter them while they're hot, put the bottom half on a plate and spread it generously with berries (which have been standing in honey long enough to have made some juice), replace the top half of the biscuit, cover the whole with juice and whipped cream, and serve. This is guaranteed to run up your bathroom scales.

Here is another dinner to serve after the children are in bed.

BISCUIT TORTONI

½ cup sugar
¾ cup rich milk
1 cup cookie crumbs—macaroon or cocoanut or shortbread
1 teaspoon almond flavoring
¼ teaspoon vanilla flavoring
1 cup whipping cream

Combine half of the crumbs with the milk, a pinch of salt, and the sugar. Let stand for an hour or two, then fold in the whipped cream and flavoring. You can pour it into custard cups if you like; I prefer a large bowl. In either case, sprinkle the remaining crumbs on top. Put in freezing chamber for three hours or more.

If you serve it by putting the big bowl on the table, however few your guests you won't have any left over, although it is supposed to be enough for eight servings.

And now a little invention of my own which enjoys some popularity.

IMOGEN PUDDING

Crumble into a baking dish some dried left-over cookies or cake which no one in the family seems to be willing to eat, and add honey to taste. Add any fruit on hand if it's juicy: applesauce, rhubarb, canned or frozen peaches, cherries, prunes. If there isn't enough juice in the fruit to make the dish quite moist, add water or milk or cream, according to your diet and pocketbook. Water, with honey or syrup added, is plenty good enough. Put in raisins, currants, figs, or dates if desired. And nuts; they contribute glamor, and if you put in enough so that each person will get two or three, that will answer.

Bake this in a slow oven for perhaps fifteen minutes; it should not be too moist but it mustn't be dry. Serve with or without cream, plain or whipped.

When this turns out to be particularly good, I will unfortunately probably never be able to repeat it, not having the same things around again all at once. Also, I never can quite remember what I put into it.

Do you like bananas and cream? Try adding some maple syrup to them.

As for coffee, we buy it green and roast our own, which is very little trouble, for we have a small electric roaster which does the job while I go about other business. We like the freshness of our coffee very much but I wouldn't try to convert anyone to this method, chiefly because I doubt if you could find an electric roaster; we seem to have bought the last one in existence. Instant coffee is of course a handy thing to have on tap. But I don't believe it's so much simpler than brewing it, as we do, in an electric pot which stops automatically when the coffee is ready, then keeps it hot. At least you don't have to jump up at dessert time and go to the kitchen and boil water, as you would for instant coffee. Doing it our way, of course the coffee pot has to be washed and the grounds disposed of, but if you live in the country you probably know that the grounds are splendid mulch for any outdoor plant, and if you live in the city and have house plants you can put some of the grounds in their pots.

Please don't think I am trying to tell you that instant coffee has an inferior flavor; you know what tastes good to you. One of our friends always brings his own instant coffee with him when he comes here for a weekend, for the simple reason that he prefers it to our freshly roasted brew. But we're broad-minded; we don't despise him for this, we're just sorry for him.

Holidays are, of course, peak times for entertaining. Let's consider one that is often the most harrowing, just because it has come to be centered around food: Thanksgiving. Well, of all the meals of the year our Thanksgiving dinner is one of the easiest to prepare and serve, and we've had the same guests on this holiday ever since we were married.

That morning I bring turnips and carrots in from the garden, scrub them and put them in the refrigerator. These friends like raw things with their cocktails, and as soon as they arrive Helene will peel the turnips, cut them and the carrots into slender strips and arrange them, with assorted crackers and nuts, on one of the large wooden canapé platters which Fred makes. I don't do this job beforehand partly because we are told not to lose vitamins by cutting up vegetables before we're ready to eat them, and partly because Helene enjoys making a work of art of them.

I don't have to give the other vegetables a thought until the cocktails are finished: they are in the freezer. The last time I had stewed pumpkin. It's surprising how many people, even those who grow them, never use pumpkin as a vegetable. Practically everyone to whom I've served stewed pumpkin asks if it's winter squash or sweet potato, and I've yet to find anyone who didn't like it. Here's the recipe, which you might like to try:

STEWED MASHED PUMPKIN OR WINTER SQUASH

Don't use a huge Hallowe'en job if you can get a small sugar pumpkin. Or butternut, buttercup, or Blue Hubbard squash. Or if you will cook pumpkin and squash together, I think you will like it, because pumpkin is rather watery and squash quite dry.

I find that the easiest way to handle a squash is to first cut it in half with a heavy sharp knife, and then cut into slices; this makes it easy to peel. Remove the seeds, and if you dry those of either pumpkin or Blue Hubbard and eat them the way you do sunflower seeds (or don't you?), you may find that you like them very much. I believe they are also supposed to be good for you, but don't hold that against them until you have given them a fair trial.

Now peel, then cut into rather small pieces, so that it will cook quickly. Put it on low heat; you don't need to use any water if you watch it carefully; it will very soon make enough liquid itself to keep it from burning.

When it's tender I mash it, then cook it a few minutes longer with the lid off if it's at all watery. If there's more liquid than will evaporate in a few minutes, I pour it off and drink it (because of its vitamin content). The more nearly I can achieve the consistency of mashed sweet potatoes, the better our guests seem to like it.

Now salt it a little and add brown sugar and grated nutmeg. Then, the last minute, add butter and sweet or sour cream. Don't use enough cream to make it watery; or you can omit either the butter or cream, but not both.

This vegetable is just as good after having been in the refrigerator a few days as it is the day you cook it.

For the other vegetable I had cole slaw. It took me many years to learn how to make this dish tempting; now people really seem to like my recipe, so I'll give it to you.

COLE SLAW

Put the head of cabbage (a solid one) into the refrigerator hours, or even days, before shredding it. Then, about two hours before you expect to serve, slice it into long thin shreds. Put this into a large wooden bowl and add soybean oil. It is less expensive than olive oil, we like it better, and it is supposed to be better for you. Toss thoroughly. Then add about one half as much vinegar as oil, and generous sprinklings of dehydrated onion and spiced salt and some pepper. Squeeze in the juice from a clove of garlic. Toss very thoroughly again and taste.

Put it into the bowl you will serve it in and set in a cool place.

A good many men like to skip the salad, and often eat it only from a sense of duty. When you pin them down you may find that they like the taste but hate the bother of eating it. For a tossed green salad I don't know what you can do about this, because even when the pieces are quite small it's still rather a messy thing to eat. You could, of course, serve it first—almost any hungry man will eat salad rather than just sit and watch other people eat. But that seems rather a mean trick. Cole slaw, which is easy to eat, may be a better solution.

It is now almost one o'clock and our Thanksgiving company will arrive any minute; am I ready for them?

Canapés: Helene will attend to them.

Cocktails: Fred's department, and always ready.

Turkey: I just checked the thermometer; it is done.

Homemade grape jam: we serve this instead of cranberry sauce.

Cole slaw: ready.

Pumpkin: ready except for heating.

Stuffing: there is lots of this so we don't have potatoes, and it's ready, of course, inside the turkey.

Dessert: if our guests didn't bring it, as they traditionally do, it would have been a simple matter of filling and baking one of the pie crusts ready and waiting in the freezer. And that's another advantage of slow-roasting: you can take the roast out of the oven, bake a pie, put the roast back in and no harm done.

I can believe that my dinner may seem skimpy to many of

you; where are the traditional mashed turnips, creamed onions, celery, potatoes? All right, the woman who loves to prepare a large meal on a holiday has a fine time, I'm sure, and I'm all for anyone doing what she enjoys, if it isn't too hard on her and the people around. But for you who wear yourselves out at such a time just for the sake of tradition, or because you think your family and company will be happier with a great variety of food set before them—well, I wish you would think it over. Or even put it to a vote next time.

Naturally I can't speak for anyone else's family and friends but I think I can for mine: I know Fred wouldn't want me wrestling with food for long hours merely for the sake of serving an elaborate holiday dinner. And as for our annual Thanksgiving guests, if I hardly had time to greet them when they arrived and, instead of having a drink with them, hovered over the stove making gravy, mashing potatoes, and doing countless other last-minute chores, I know that they would be uncomfortable and might even hesitate to accept our invitation each year. Most people don't want anyone to overdo in order to prepare more food for them than they either need or want.

As it is, we gather in the living room for a pleasant time together. When Helene, Ada and I eventually go to the kitchen, we take Albert along to carve. He distributes the turkey on the plates, Helene adds the stuffing and pumpkin, Ada takes the plates to the table. Thinking hard, I don't seem to be able to scare up anything for *me* to do; oh, yes, bring out the cole slaw. Fred pours the wine. Doesn't Herbert do anything? Certainly. He tells me that I look younger than I did a year ago, and my guess is that that's the only lie he indulges in from one Thanksgiving to another.

Incidentally, speaking of wine, I imagine you may follow the rules (particularly if you have guests), but if, for instance, you're having beef and you yourself prefer white wine with it instead of red, here's hoping that you go ahead and put a glass of the white at your place. Not in defiance, but as casually as you might drink water while others were having ginger ale. It's another trifle, but if we can learn to be ourselves in one small thing without strain, then I feel sure that we soon can do the same in important things.

I've no reason to doubt that some of the people who can't bear a wrong combination shudder legitimately. And since we poor mortals are so unsure of ourselves that we'll use any sort of excuse to look down on our fellow beings, these people often snatch this opportunity to feel above the rest of us. Well, let them, if it comforts them. Let a host of people look down on you for a host of reasons just as long as you don't allow them to trick you into looking up to them.

It seems to me the surest cure for feeling either superior or inferior to our fellows is the realization that all of us, from the worst to the best, are rather helpless, groping creatures blunderingly doing the best we can with the combination of heritage and environment which was wished on us. I realize that this is primarily a subject for the psychiatrists and parsons, not for the cook, but I do want to add one more thought: it is obvious that feeling inferior isn't a happy sensation, but I believe that feeling superior to others is also an unpleasant frame of mind. It involves criticism, and we are surely happier when thinking of someone we like and admire than we are when thinking of someone with flaws to pick at. Now let the specialists take it from there.

You can explain until you're hoarse, and also exhausted, but you can never get it through some people's heads that it isn't a lack of love for them which makes you prefer that they let you know when they're planning to come to see you. I wrote a book about guests in which I put my cards on the table concerning this delicate subject. Since then fewer friends drop in unannounced but I'm afraid there are some vaguely hurt feelings.

Well, here's something to cheer up those who think my attitude is unreasonable, and I'm sure it does secretly please quite a few people although they pretend to sympathize with me. About five years ago I wrote a book describing my revolutionary method of gardening: no plowing, hoeing, weeding, cultivating or watering, and a whole flock of other advantages. One result of this is that so far fifteen hundred eager beavers have come to have a look at this labor-saving method and to get some pointers, and an overwhelming percentage of them have driven in without advance notice.

In my garden a number of vegetables may be invisible but coming up under the hay which covers the patch, so Fred put up a sign at the entrance, aimed to keep people from walking all over everything when we're not at home. It reads:

Fools Rush In—Be an Angel and Stay Out of the Garden

This past five years' experience has confirmed two opinions I have had for some time about human beings in general and unexpected visitors in particular. One is that people, by and large, are well-equipped with the wish to be considerate of others, even if they can't swing it. I believe that they often fail because they are short on imagination; very few of us can put ourselves in the other person's place and act accordingly.

Anyhow, whether we like it or not, once in a while someone

is going to drop in unexpectedly at mealtime. Such a person falls into one of two categories: we are glad to see him or we wish he had gone someplace where he would have been welcome. There is hardly a thing we can do about this second brand except to be insincerely cordial—unless it is to keep some uninspiring cans of food in the house to discourage him from repeating the performance. Cans of pork and beans, clam chowder, chili con carne, spaghetti in tomato sauce would be my choice. These are all things which I myself eat with reluctance, but the catch is that our uninvited callers may like them. It would of course be more effective to find out what particular foods these people dislike and keep them all in stock, but this seems like taking too much trouble for the satisfaction of being disagreeable. But if you like these people who just popped in well enough to want to give them something acceptable, here's a quick and easy dish.

CLAMS WITH CREAM

2 cans of clams	1 pint light cream
2 onions	1 pint milk
2 tablespoons flour	Salt pork

Cut the pork into small pieces and fry until brown. Then fry the onions until yellow, add flour, cream, milk, and clam juice. Cook a few minutes, then add the clams and heat, but don't boil.

Butter will do instead of the pork. You can always have canned clams on hand; the minced ones are a good deal cheaper than the whole ones, and we prefer them. I always have some cream in the freezer, so I'm never out of the makings for this dish. Perhaps evaporated milk would do if you have no cream on hand. Sometimes we have this for the main dinner dish, in which case I usually add potatoes.

And here's another concoction for the preferred kind of unexpected guest. If you will keep on hand some eggs, some cans of bean sprouts, onions and canned shrimp or chicken, you will always have the ingredients for this and the recipe is on the can of sprouts. However, I rarely use sprouts any more, for Fred and I both like the dish better with the various vegetables I have substituted for them.

EGG FOO YUNG

Sauté three or four medium-sized onions along with green pepper or cabbage or summer squash or kohlrabi or asparagus or peas or any combination of those vegetables. Undercook them a little; they should be on the crisp side. Add shrimp or chicken or pork or ham, as much or as little as you like. (If your people are meat eaters, the dish will taste better to them if you're generous.) Shake in some soy sauce. Cool. When ready to fry it, add two eggs for each person.

I heat two small iron skillets, put in some pork drippings, bacon grease, or soybean oil, and fry a large spoonful of the mixture in each skillet, which I keep medium hot. If the first two cakes more or less fall to pieces when you turn them, you have too much vegetable for the amount of egg; add one or two more eggs. Serve it with soy sauce.

I can't give you quantities on this; I can only tell you that I use more vegetables than seems reasonable, much more than the recipe on the bean sprout can calls for. I do this because

Fred and I are so fond of this dish that, except for dessert, we make a dinner of it.

You can cook the vegetables in the morning, then all you have to do at dinnertime is fry the omelets. It takes about twenty minutes to do a platterful for us two.

Once at lunchtime some friends drove in just as Fred and I were sitting down to liverwurst sandwiches and milk. I liked these people well enough to go to a little trouble, so I heated a can of tomatoes, adding a few slices of dried bread (fresh bread will do) to take up the juice and seasoning it with salt, pepper, brown sugar, butter. While the tomatoes heated, I sliced some liverwurst (fortunately there was plenty) not too thinly, put just a little fat into the skillet, and browned the meat. Company or not, you should try that sometime.

And here's a universally popular number—in fact, don't serve it to anyone unless you're willing to have him show up again soon at mealtime.

PORK SAUSAGES WITH MUSHROOMS

Cut link pork sausages into inch-length pieces and fry them. Pour off the grease (sausage grease makes lots of things taste better, so save it), add mushrooms, either fresh or canned, and cook a few minutes. Then just before you're ready to serve, add sour cream and sherry. I can't tell you how much of either of these; the amount of cream (you can use sweet cream if you prefer) depends on how much liquid you want, the amount of sherry on how strongly you want the dish to taste of it. You can even skip the sherry if you want to, or use white wine.

This is an excellent company lunch dish, and sometimes Fred and I have it for dinner. It is especially satisfactory served on toast, which has a wonderful taste when soaked with the sauce.

One of my favorite easy and quick dishes is—well, let's call it:

CHEESE WITH ANYTHING

All you need to have on hand is Cheddar cheese and almost any vegetable. Cut up some cheese, add it to the cooked vegetable and let it slowly melt. Put it into a greased casserole dish, cover with dry prepared stuffing and some more cheese, and brown slowly under the broiler. Or you can put just the vegetable in the casserole, stir in the cut-up cheese and let it melt in the oven, then add the stuffing. Easiest of all, omit the casserole dish entirely; just complete the performance on top of the stove, in the vessel in which you warmed up or steamed the vegetable. In this case, omit the stuffing.

I think I've tried this with everything except carrots, beets, squash, and tomatoes. It's especially good with peas, asparagus, and all the cabbage family.

If you're the kind of person who usually has a lot of left-overs in the refrigerator and have a talent for making something tempting out of them, you can often concoct an acceptable dish for the unexpected guest. My mother wasn't a very good cook but she was a genius with left-overs, and I think I got a little of her talent; at least I seem to be better at throwing this and that together than I am when I start from scratch.

Now, what to do about guests who are fussy eaters? If I know they are taking reducing seriously, I of course don't give them a meal which contains much fat and starch, and I don't finish off with a biscuit tortoni; that's relatively simple. If just one guest can't eat any fat at all, and I don't want to penalize the others, I give the unfortunate one cold sliced turkey which I usually have in the freezer, partly for such emergencies. It's easy to put a portion of whatever vegetable I'm serving into a small dish for him before I put butter on it, and to fix some salad without any oil. Not much fun for him, I'm afraid, and maybe he would prefer to cheat a little, but if anyone feels that certain foods are bad for him, I'm not going to be the guilty provider.

Vegetarians, entertained alone, are no problem; the cheese dish, above, is ideal for them, and there are many other substitutes for meat which are good. But if there are other guests this isn't likely to be satisfactory; most people don't go for a dinner without meat, and since everyone would know who's the cause of this meatless meal, the vegetarian might feel a little self-conscious. (I myself was one for ten years but I gave it up, primarily because I was such a pain in the neck to my hostesses.) It seems to me the most satisfactory way to treat a vegetarian is just to have plenty of other food and perhaps supply an unobtrusive bit of cheese on an individual dish.

I carefully avoid serving a meal for company that involves much running back and forth to the kitchen. Few people like to dash about during a meal, and if the hostess is doing it, the guests will probably feel uneasy because they aren't helping, or will be wondering whether or not they should help, or will just dash about with the hostess. I think all three alternatives are undesirable, so I rarely serve soup; just two courses, the main one and dessert and coffee.

When the meal is over, do you do the dishes, with or without help, or let them wait? With me it depends on my mood, and on whether or not my guests are young and vigorous or old and worn out, and on how young I myself feel at the moment. If the company is staying all night, the dishes are washed, willy-nilly. If you have an electric dishwasher I would be the last one to try to persuade you that you've wasted your money; who wants to feel cheated? And I probably couldn't convince you anyway. But if you haven't one and wish you had, I suggest you set your heart on something else. After exhaustive research (that is, watching various friends perform with their dish-washers), I've concluded that the only service this gadget renders is the provision of ample space in which to stack the dishes. A bit of a waste of money, I would say.

In any case, washing the dishes is like all the other jobs we are obliged to do. It can be as agreeable or disagreeable a chore as we choose to make it.

Now the guests have gone home, or have gone upstairs to bed. If you invited them to enjoy them, if you didn't wear yourself out before they came, didn't rush about after they arrived, didn't serve a meal so costly that the housekeeping budget is a shambles, you can lay your head on your pillow with a sigh of contentment rather than with the feeling of "Well, thank goodness *that's* over!"

VI

Once Over Lightly

In one respect, at least, there are no privileged people: each and everyone's days are equipped with twenty-four hours. It is true that we can mess up another person's time, exploit him, make him miserable, but, busy and ingenious as some people are in thinking up ways of taking advantage of their fellow-beings, no one has yet been able to figure out how to actually subtract hours from someone else's days and add them to his own. As far as the amount of time is concerned, your day is intact, and to a greater or lesser degree many of us can decide what we will do with some of those hours.

Unfortunately, this is almost a losing battle for a housewife because no one seems to have much respect for her time. She may have children, do all of her housework and cooking, care for a garden, do some sewing, and even presume to have a small hobby, yet family, friends and neighbors see nothing wrong about interrupting her in the middle of anything she may be doing. They expect some attention, too, and even a little courtesy.

These women who stay at home are earning their living as definitely as those who go to a job and receive a salary. More than that, much of their work has to be done today, and on time; the baby must be fed, the meals have to be prepared, and the beds *should* be made. If anyone feels free to make demands on them, it isn't because they have nothing to do. Is it because we feel that work done at home—washing, ironing, sweeping, cooking and so on—isn't very important?

Some people like to be interrupted, and I am sorry for them, because this surely means that they are bored with whatever they are doing and welcome anything to break the monotony. Yet I have never been able to understand how keeping house got its reputation for being duller than almost any other job. I've had various occupations—telephone operator, baby nurse, bookkeeper, salesgirl, typist, factory worker, secretary, business manager—and being as objective and honest as possible, I feel that gardening and housekeeping offer the best opportunity for avoiding monotony, because in them there is more possibility of choice than in any of the others. Except for getting the meals, making the beds, and picking the vegetables before they are over-ripe, there is considerable elasticity. Are you washing windows, and getting a little fed up with the job? Well, why not abandon that project for the time being and scrub the floor?

Or cheat for half an hour and sit down and read. Unless you are grimly determined to hate all housework and are convinced that it is deadly dull, I don't see why you can't easily work out a system and adopt an attitude which will relieve the monotony.

With most jobs away from home, this isn't so easy. For one thing, there is usually a boss around. For another, your work is likely to consist of just one kind of activity; no such welcome freedom as switching from ironing to baking. You post figures in a ledger, or you type, or stand all day behind a counter and wait on people, or say "Number, please" over and over. I can't make out why housework should seem less inspiring than any of those activities. (But come to think of it, I didn't find them dull either.) Even if you are a Big Shot—a Career Woman who is her own boss—it isn't all peaches and cream. You may not be bored, but my guess is that you will be more or less hectic.

We hear it claimed that a man is lucky because he goes to an office or shop or factory every day while the poor little woman has to stay at home and do the housework, which is called drudgery. Her life is considered very dull, by comparison, and in no sense broadening. To my mind that notion is nonsense. You either have it in you to "broaden" or you don't, and it doesn't matter much where you are; even on a desert island you could probably learn a few things if you put your mind to it.

If you have a job you must get up and face the new day when the clock tells you to. You probably have a hurried breakfast (no lingering, as the housewife may), then dash to the bus or subway. On your way you have a chance to observe those around you or even to get into a conversation with the person next to you and do a little "broadening," but I have seldom seen anyone take advantage of this splendid opportunity. Most of the passengers read; the others sit or stand silently, looking sleepy or bored or both. When you arrive at your place of business you will no doubt find that there is enough work to keep you occupied, but it is rarely fascinating, and even if it gives you opportunities to study human nature you are likely to get to the point where you wish you could take your fellow creatures in smaller doses. At lunchtime you may wish you could trade a crowded restaurant for a quiet hour at home with a sandwich and a glass of milk. And at closing time, probably in a conveyance too full of other people, you hurry home to a period of rest and "stagnation."

The woman who stays at home (first we will take those without children) can relax over another cup of coffee after her husband has gone. There may be plenty of work to be done but she's her own boss. She will no doubt wash the dishes, make the beds and get the dinner in the evening, but beyond that the way she spends the day is to a great extent a matter of mood and conscience. It seems obvious to me that a housewife who has no children, and no compulsion to be a slave to her home, has ample time to go out among people and observe them, to visit museums or attend a lecture or read something "broadening." And if she hasn't it in her to do these things while she is "merely" a housewife, how could she possibly manage to get any of them done if she sat at a desk or stood behind a counter all day?

If you are a mother, you have, in a manner of speaking, as many bosses as you have children, and they aren't likely to let you soldier on the job. You are tied down, it's true, but I fail to see why it is more broadening, for example, to type somebody else's letters than it is to watch a child's mind develop. If, that is, you *permit* it to develop.

But the choice of how to occupy her time is to a large extent denied the meticulous housekeeper. *Her* work handles *her,* and she often has a strained look, almost as tense and driven as the overworked head of a firm. Doesn't it stand to reason that, in this dusty world, any housekeeper who won't tolerate the presence of any dirt at any time has to be too alert for her own good? If you are one of these and are so skillful at rationalizing that you have convinced yourself that the end justifies the means, waste no time on the following (to you) nonsense; you will be much happier tackling some (to me) already clean cupboard.

Now I am certainly not going to say arbitrarily that doing this or that around the house isn't worth the bother; how do I know whether it is or not for you? And of course I'm not talking to the women who thoroughly *enjoy* keeping a house spotless. *All* I am trying to do is throw out the lifeline to anyone who is being tossed about in a sea of housework and isn't liking it much.

If, for instance, you hate to clean, yet can't bear to see dust around or even to know there's some under the couch, it's just possible you will find something in the following pages that will lighten your labors somewhat; I hope so. I may be able to give a few hints to those of you who like other activities better than housework, and who may sort of let the dust over-accumulate while you vaguely wish you didn't. But I'm not going to try to persuade you to let the dust lie there safely for a while longer if it bothers you.

First of all, I beg those who loathe housework to watch their thinking, and I have Shakespeare to back me up; he tells us: ". . . there is nothing either good or bad, but thinking makes it so." He didn't put this in the mouth of one of his minor characters, either; no less a person than Hamlet says it. I guess we will all agree that our attitude to anything, big or small, will help or hinder us, according to whether or not it is cheerful or gloomy, constructive or destructive. It is probably true that every time we say "I loathe housework" we add to our distaste for it. It follows, then, unless we like to hate the thing we're obliged to do, it's a little foolish to keep rubbing it in. If it makes you feel ridiculous to replace that thought with "I love housework" (when goodness knows you don't), you might try shutting it out with a neutral one, such as "The days are getting longer, spring will soon be here," or "Everybody seemed to have a fine time last night; looks as if I'm a good hostess." Of course if they had a dull time you'll have to look around for some other cheering thought.

It isn't easy always to control one's thinking, but those of you who hate to dust might try saying to yourselves, "How much better everything looks with a little attention!" rather than "You're never through; you dust today but what for? Everything will need it again before I get my breath." Both are true, but one thought is pleasant and the other isn't, and you do have a choice. If you are deciding among several dresses all the same price, or two different people to visit, surely there is a screw loose somewhere if, everything being equal, you pick the one you like least. We can't always have the dress or the companion we prefer, but did you ever stop to think that nothing on earth but yourself can keep you from having the very finest thoughts you are capable of imagining?

One friend, knowing I was writing this book, said, "Whatever else you say, tell people to work with a schedule. You never get anything done if you don't stick to a routine." Another advised me, "If you're going to try to show women how not to mind housework, be sure to tell them never to plan ahead, but to do things when they feel like it. Routine will drive anyone crazy."

Two women with different temperaments, and how futile it would be to suggest to either one of them that she should change! And a pity, too, if she should attempt it, for although I hope and believe that each one of us can make some improvement in our behavior, character, way of living, if we care enough to put our minds to it, I doubt the wisdom of trying to radically revise our natural inclinations.

I happen to like to work with a schedule, which I call rhythm to keep it from sounding dull. On the other hand, one of my sisters hates routine; therefore luckily I have known for most of my life that there's no system that suits everyone. The result is that I'm not in the least tempted to try to convince anyone that my way is best just because it happens to suit me. I wouldn't even ask anyone to give it a trial. I am convinced, however, that there are a large number of housewives who would like to be more casual about their work but who are consciously or unconsciously afraid of criticism; they might appreciate a little backing, and that's the main thing I'm trying to give them.

If you are in the habit of giving the whole house a thorough cleaning once a week and hate looking forward to that day, you might try this: divide the work into five parts, or six, if you are willing to include Saturday. It's true that by this system the house is never all clean at once, but it's never all dirty at once either. And then use your judgment. In every room there are a few strategic spots which tell the tale: a table, a lamp, a mirror. With a cloth handy these can be kept clean and the rest of the room can await your mood. Assuming that you are doing this for the esthetic satisfaction of yourself and family, all you need do until cleaning day comes again (and it will soon be here, you can count on that) is to tidy the things the eye is most apt to fall on.

One of the most important words in the English language is that little one: why? I can't think of anything more sensational than a "Why Week" would be if people forced themselves to give a reasonable answer for everything they did, and acted accordingly. Why do men wear strips of cloth under their collars? Why do we buy candy and soft drinks for our children when dentists agree that they harm teeth? Why do we buy a new car when the old one is doing fine? Why do I invite her to my home although I don't much like her? Shall we sit down in our living rooms and look carefully around and question a few things? It will be surprising if there isn't at least one object in the room that has no function, no value either sentimental or monetary, and isn't very attractive. You may even vaguely dislike it, once you stop to give it a critical look, yet you have been faithfully dusting it week in, week out, for years.

Ideally, I suppose that everything around that has to be dusted should pay for this service by being both beautiful and useful. As I look over our living room I see that it's not ideal in that respect. The three Delft vases on top of the highboy have no utilitarian value; however, they are up so high that you can't see the dust on them (at least I can't). I have to use a small ladder to reach them, so it's their fate not to get cleaned very often. The handsome samovar has been used only three or four times in twenty years; the brass Sabbath lamp, hanging in the corner, is useless and a nuisance to dust, too, if you take the job seriously. We never light the candles in the tall Chinese candlesticks on the curio cabinet; the porcelain birds on the loudspeaker cabinet never sing. And there's one little number over on a wall cupboard whose continued presence there baffles me; it is a small brass ikon which I brought back from Russia. Its sentimental value is negligible, and it is constantly falling over. Why does this person who is so competent at evading unnecessary labor that she even writes books about it leave that ikon there to be dusted? I have no idea. Anybody want it?

Our newest useless thing is a fish which Fred carved recently; it is on a stand between the candlesticks and, since my eyesight isn't perfect, from across the room it looks to me more like a large bird standing on one leg than a fish. But whichever it looks like I don't mind dusting it, because it is graceful and charming. And that's it for our living room. For one the size of ours there are relatively few things sitting around in idleness, and I've decided that these are worth what little attention they get.

As for trying to keep a house spotless, how can one do this without showing some minor agony if someone comes in with dirty shoes, or if cigarette ashes are inadvertently spilled, and so on and on? And a room where not one object is out of place, where every cushion on the couch is arranged with mathematical precision, and the magazines and books on the table are always just so—well, this has to mean one of two things: either someone must be constantly going around putting things back in order, or no one is allowed to toss anything down casually. I feel a sort of tension and strain behind anything carried to such lengths.

The other extreme, either in uncleanliness or disorder, is as bad, if not worse. Dust lying quietly and contentedly under a couch or bed, waiting for cleaning day, is one thing; it doesn't offend the eye and won't contaminate anything else, so what is so wrong about leaving it there a while longer? Even a reasonable amount of dust on the legs of chairs seems inoffensive; who goes about inspecting chair legs? Only those visitors, I should think, who would like to find out for sure what they already suspect: that you aren't a very good housekeeper. And it would seem rather mean to show them that they are mistaken; nobody likes to be wrong.

But I believe that a constantly cluttered and dusty house is hard on us, even though we may not realize it. Keeping conspicuous and strategic places wiped off takes very little time. And a reasonable amount of order is more time-saving than disorder, once you establish it. Someone once told me that she was neat because she was lazy; untidiness took too much energy in trying to find things.

I can't think of a single constructive word to say to those women whose homes are almost constantly dirty and cluttered. I believe that modern psychology has put such housekeepers down as neurotics, along with the over-immaculate ones. All I can add is that I am truly sorry for both over-dirty and over-clean people. And either kind must be hard to live with.

Cleaning a reasonable number of things that have no utilitarian value doesn't seem to me too high a price to pay if they are a pleasure to have around, but not for anything would I bother with curtains: put them up, take them down, wash and iron them, hang them up again. Our not very large house has twenty windows, and the state institution for the unbalanced is the place for me if I ever get far enough gone to cover them with curtains. (The institution is handy, only about ten miles from us.)

Our windows are the old-fashioned kind with small panes and narrow frames and, quite aside from the work involved, for my taste they are more attractive without curtains than they would be with them. If I were unlucky enough to have big ugly windows which cried for curtains I would be in a major predicament. Anyhow, it might be worth your while to give a thought, with the keynote *Why?*, to your own curtain situation.

Now about rugs. Even before I had read what Thoreau had to say against them I had decided they were expendable. Then, as you may remember, a few years ago a famous lady said her little piece on the subject in a very successful book. As I recall, she went off to a beach for a vacation, discovered it was easier to clean the house if you didn't have a rug on the floor, and took hers up. But since she said nothing about discarding her rugs when she was back at home again, perhaps it's safe to assume that she didn't. Therefore, what she found out at the beach didn't impress me, since surely everybody already knew that rugs make work, and since probably most people have enough imagination to do without them during a vacation at the beach.

I guess it's a safe bet that you won't discard your rugs because of the way *I* feel about them, and certainly there's no reason why you should as long as you're happy spending money buying them and time keeping them clean. But again you might pause to consider whether they are more of a nuisance than a comfort to you. In our living room (twenty-two by eighteen feet) there is no rug down for nine months of the year. The floor boards are old and wide and, to me, attractive. During the three winter months we put down one rug (six by nine), but off to the side where there isn't much traffic, so that anyone who may come in with wet or dirty shoes needn't walk on it. Why do I put it down at all? Well, the chief reason is that Fred seems to like a rug on the floor in winter, and the little time I spend running the vacuum over it isn't much of a sacrifice at that time of year when I can probably do with a little more exercise than I might otherwise get.

There are no rugs in our upstairs rooms. Fred and I put on slippers as we get out of bed, so I can think of no good reason for rugs in our bedrooms. But shouldn't guests be catered to, treated with consideration? By all means, I once decided, and dug out two small rugs (which I had hung onto, just in case) and put one in front of each bed in the guest room. I don't remember how long they were kept on the floor. Maybe a year or two. Then one fine day in early spring, as I shook them out of the bedroom window instead of using the vacuum (no doubt getting my hair full of dust), the row of roses below stared up at me and cried out; "What on earth do you think you're doing? What are you accomplishing? Don't you know that it's high time to prune us? If you had any . . ."

I couldn't hear the rest because of the uproar from every other flower, every blade of grass and even the entire vegetable garden, all shouting in derision at that silly creature who was spending her time shaking dirt out of a piece of cloth, only to put it back on the floor and walk on it and get it dusty again. Especially when there were so many things to be done outside which were so much more fascinating and constructive.

One thing any house is inevitably full of is walls, and kitchen walls especially seem to demand attention. Do you wash them yourself? I did, for quite a few years, choosing a time for it during the winter months, when the garden wasn't calling me. And worse than the walls was the ceiling. I think every brand of soap powder and cleanser ever manufactured has dripped, at one time or another, onto my head. I tried brushes, long-handled mops, cloths. I risked my life on stepladders. But I wouldn't have minded any of it very much (after all, you can face almost anything once a year) if only the ceiling had looked any different when I got through.

One day, five or six years ago, a neighbor came to deliver milk just as I had finished one half of the job, and I asked him, "Art, can you tell which part of the ceiling I've washed?"

He made a careful survey, then picked the wrong half. What a break! I didn't do the other half and have never washed the ceiling since. Painting it will have to answer from now on, and that isn't my department, I'm glad to say.

Kitchens have other hazards, of course. Most notably the stove. Cleaning a greasy oven is a job I've always disliked, and I fell for every kind of "easy" grease remover on the market. Some even claimed to be miraculous. Not one was what I would call easy and not one miracle among them all. To some slight extent I manage to follow the splendid advice I give others, and as I work away on the oven I am usually able to tell myself cheerfully, "This job isn't *really* such a pain in the neck." But if I happen to be in a defeated mood, when frost has just killed the tomato plants, for instance, I am more than likely to catch myself fuming, "It's still greasy! Wouldn't you think that eventually . . ."

Actually our stove is old enough to retire, oven and all. The electrician who comes to fix something on it once in a while always exclaims over its antiquity and tries to shame us into buying a new one. But this one still performs satisfactorily and I'm even quite attached to it. We have grown old together, my stove and I, and we are both a little more battered-looking than we once were, and less shining, but we are still able to do our jobs adequately enough. I think it would be unfair and inconsiderate to throw me on the junk heap when I can still pretty well hold up my end of things, and I don't think my stove deserves that fate yet, either.

Our kitchen floor is hardwood and it is varnished once a year, which makes it easy to clean. I find that it looks all right with less frequent scrubbing than did the linoleum which we once had. I happen to like to scrub a kitchen, perhaps because it's an open-and-shut case; unlike dusting a room or cooking a meal, there's no skipping and no fancy touches. You simply wash every foot of it and the deal is terminated. But I try not to do it so often that the task becomes boring. Also, it seems a little inconsiderate to keep your floor so immaculate that the laundryman, milkman, plumber, not to mention your friends, would feel diffident about stepping in on a rainy day.

As I finished writing that last sentence I remembered something that happened when I was a child. Our neighbors had just slaughtered a hog and their two little girls brought us a piece of it for a present, and also some for my grandparents who lived not far beyond us. It's fun to give presents, as anyone knows, so of course I was eager to go with them to Grandma's and enjoy the surprise and delight on her face when they gave her the meat.

It had rained the night before and the country road was muddy. As the three of us approached the back door (we knew better than to go in the front way in our dirty shoes), Grandma opened it and snapped: "Don't come up on the porch with your muddy feet."

I was horribly embarrassed. These were my friends, bringing a present to my Grandma, and all she could think of was her old porch. It didn't help at all that she acted pleased about the gift and gave us a lot of cookies. I feel sure that that incident had much to do with my feeling that there is something out of balance when anyone puts too big an emphasis on keeping a place immaculate.

For my taste, nothing decorates a room more effectively than open shelves of books, yet nobody can dispute the fact that they gather dust, and dusting even a few hundred volumes (we had about five thousand books around when I was growing up) is a long and tedious job. It's true that the dust on books doesn't show, at least not much, and if you don't mind knowing it's there, fine. But then I have seen many a person take a book from a shelf and blow the dust off the top. While I'm far from a fussy housekeeper, I never have been in favor of blowing dust off of anything; it certainly is going to land somewhere, probably on me.

If books aren't a bothersome cleaning problem for you and you enjoy having them around, by all means fill your shelves. But if you are simply trying to impress people with your collection, or are hoarding books as some hoard money, then consider that you are perhaps being selfish, that they might serve a better purpose if passed along to others. The money misers do have one advantage, incidentally; they don't have to dust their collection.

I mentioned windows before, in connection with curtains. Now let's look at them bare. Besides the twenty windows in the rooms of our house, there are nineteen others, in storeroom, pantry, porch. But that isn't as much work as it sounds, because the nineteen aren't exposed to the dirt from the furnace, so they don't need washing very often, according to my standards. I have tried everything I've ever heard of that is supposed to make window-washing easy and simple, and I'm not enough sold on any one of them to recommend it. The crazy thing about it is that one product seems to work splendidly for a while, then it sort of goes back on you. Probably your enthusiasm for it at first is only by way of contrast to the disillusionment you feel about the last one you tried.

If you do it often enough, wiping the panes with cleansing tissue will keep them fairly presentable. My latest preference, however, is to wash them quickly with clear water and a rag or sponge, then with clean, very hot water and a clean rag wash them again and don't dry them. It's the drying of a window that takes the time. Done this way they look pretty good, it's over with before you know it, and energy expended is at a minimum. Sometimes I put ammonia in the water, but other times I forget.

One of my friends said the other day, "If I can't see through the window I open the door and look out." However, her windows are usually clean; only a good housekeeper would dare make a remark like that. The others avoid saying anything that would cause you to glance at their windows.

It's a matter of temperament how window-washing is handled; you may prefer to make a big job of it, doing all of them on a set day and every so often. Or perhaps you keep putting the job off until you are forced to do it, if you want to see whether or not it's raining without stepping outside. Here's a trick of mine which may possibly appeal to some of you. One morning Fred may be slow in coming down to breakfast, and instead of eating without him, or impatiently wondering what on earth is holding him up, I wash a window or two. A day or so later, I may put something on the stove to cook and have to wait around until it starts to boil, so I do another window. Before I know it, they're all washed. Of course by the time I've finished twenty by that method, the first one is asking for attention again, but at least I haven't made a big job of it and haven't had to steal some reading time.

There are two kinds of good housekeepers: those who can't stand to see any dirt around, and those who can't even bear to know it's there. If you belong to the first group, you certainly have learned the device of washing the windows where the sun shines in oftener than those, usually on the north, where the dirt doesn't show much. If you belong to the second category, you're stuck.

I don't really know of any easy out on the upkeep of bathrooms, except perhaps to choose the various materials involved sensibly and then train the family to co-operate, a subject we'll get to in a later chapter. As for beds, how much energy do you allot to them? Of course they should always be made so that they are comfortable and, since an untidily made one is unlovely, they should be neat if you or anyone sees them during the day. If no one does, I can think of no good reason for bothering with fancy spreads and other fussy touches.

In all household chores, why not use our brains to save our tired backs and aching feet? Do we feel so insignificant, are we so cowed, that we must do this and that just because others do? Or is it that we think we are so important that people are profoundly interested in how we run our households?

VII

Why the Whirlwind?

WITH nine children in our family, some ingenuity was required to keep the house reasonably neat. There was a rule that any garment, toy, or book left where it shouldn't be was put into a big old chest in the back hall. It stayed there for a week unless the owner of it was rich or desperate enough to redeem it. Since we were always pretty short of pennies and a nickel was far too sacred to waste on a mere necessity such as a pair of mittens, few things landed in the chest. We needed our clothes, we wanted our toys and dolls, and it was out of the question to wait a whole week to find out whether or not the hero managed to rescue the heroine before she suffered the "fate worse than death" at the hands of the villain. (I don't remember that I, for one, ever stopped to wonder what that fate could be; I simply took it for granted that it was to be avoided at any cost. It was true that no hero had ever failed to get there in the nick of time but you never could tell; this one just might not make it and you *had* to know.)

So Mother never had to pick up after us nor scold nor hound us into doing it ourselves. The woman who enjoys being a servant to her family, picking up the things they leave around and cleaning up after them, must be satisfied with her lot and needs no advice from anyone. But the one who does all this and scolds about it, and complains of it to her friends, or even only to herself, is surely not handling the situation efficiently. Apparently she has spoiled both her husband and children, and it seems to me there are two alternatives more desirable than the path she has chosen: one is to put her mind to it and change the thoughtless behavior of her family; the other is to realize that she has got herself into a mess she is incapable of handling, accept it, and stop resenting it.

Once Fred accused me of spoiling every man we knew except him, and my answer was, "Of course. I have to *live* with *you.*"

It is, I believe, in the nature of some women to enjoy spoiling people, to fuss over them, pamper them, do nice little things for them. Which is fine if it's done for a guest who stays for a short time, but it's a deplorable thing to do to anyone you live with; they get used to it, expect it, even demand it. Then you may get to the point where you resent the whole thing, or at least regret it. Worse than that, the chances are that you have made the ones you love most into the sort of people others aren't going to like much. If you should have the pampering urge, it might be a good idea to get hold of an animal and give it the treatment. Even that is rather a pity, but better, surely, than messing up a human being who would suffer more from it than a dog or cat is likely to do.

Some women keep their houses immaculate just for the sake of their families, and if the work is a pleasure to them and they do it cheerfully, all's well. But if they feel put upon, it might be fairly easy to find out just how much cleanliness the various members of the family would require if they were obliged to do the work themselves. The difficulty in making loose general comments is that each case is different, but if I were married to a man who went to work every day and who shared his income with me and all I had to do was keep the house in order, I would certainly do my best to have it always shining if that was what he wanted. But if we both went to jobs, or if we had children, or if in some way I contributed to our income and worked as long hours as he did, I wouldn't feel that I was being unfair if I made very little attempt to live up to all the high standards of housekeeping that he might think up.

One thing seems clear and reasonable to me: if you're stuck with something you hate, and can't get out of it, and feel it's unjust, you have the right to cry on any shoulder you can borrow. Better not do it too frequently, though—just often enough to give you some relief. But I have known housekeepers who overwork, hate it, complain about it, are cranky and even furious with their husbands on account of it, yet when pinned down admit that they are doing more than anybody, particularly the poor husband, wants or expects them to do. It's they themselves who *must* have things just so, but they blame everyone except themselves for being always tired. I would call this unreasonable. If, on the other hand, your family's standard of cleanliness is higher than your own, you still don't have to go to extremes in order to keep them happy. If any one of them is going to crawl under the furniture to find out whether or not you're doing your duty, he deserves to come out covered with dust balls.

There's one kind of housekeeper I'm truly sorry for: the sort who has kept her place spotless for some forty or fifty years, who is still wearing herself out at it and would love to let down a little, but feels obliged to live up to her reputation. A good reputation can be a terrible slave driver. I know a woman who is past seventy and not very well, yet she scrubs and cleans and polishes her place every day and is always tired and wishes she could take it easier but doesn't dare. And it isn't her family, it's her friends who have her stymied. I, for one, will never egg her on by mentioning how shining her house looks; I don't want that on my conscience. I don't feel that we do anyone a favor when we praise them for something that they rightly wish they could stop doing.

This thing of behaving in such-and-such a way because so-and-so expects it of us is a ticklish business. Probably all of us, consciously or not, now and then behave a little better than we feel like doing at the moment because someone who cares for us would be disappointed in us otherwise. I have an idea that this is a good and helpful procedure. But I do wish that the housekeeper who works harder than she would like to would sit down in a comfortable chair and ask herself why. Say to herself, "Do I really want a few words of approval about the appearance of this house desperately enough to pay so high a price? Is there so little else in me to commend that I must keep my house shining if I am to get any praise from my friends?" If she decides that the answer is Yes, she's doomed, but if she thinks that it might be No and will try to find out, then she will no doubt have some fun with the time and energy she will soon have to spare.

When you have house guests, it may actually be doing them a favor to let the work slide while they are with you. Some years ago a woman I didn't know very well (the wife of an old friend) spent several days with us; she hadn't ever had to do a lick of housework in her life and I asked her, "Are you uncomfortable visiting someone who hasn't a maid? Do you wonder whether or not you should try to help?" (I had quickly felt so easy with her that even on such short acquaintance I could ask her that question without feeling brash).

She laughed and said, "Usually I am, but here I've never felt so relaxed in my life. You have hardly stirred off the couch since I got here."

She was exaggerating; I did give her something to eat now and then. But I was pleased that she felt no strain around her.

Spring and fall housecleaning tornadoes are special disasters for most men. If they are around the house they loathe the upset; if they go to a job they dread coming home at night to an exhausted and cranky woman. And if any of you can tackle and effectively perform this drastic job twice a year and remain relaxed, unhurried, unexhausted and in a good humor, you shouldn't be reading this book, you should be writing one. Anyhow, since I am more casual about housekeeping than their wives and don't go in for these hectic sessions, men often ask me plaintively if all the upheaval is necessary. Must a house be cleaned fundamentally from basement to attic in one or two weeks? Can't I somehow persuade their wives to do it with a less frantic tempo?

Of course there isn't a thing in the world I can do; the women are usually there to hear these pleadings, and if that doesn't soften their hearts, nothing I might say would penetrate. Besides, the wives probably feel, whether they will admit it or not, that if they can half kill themselves to provide a clean and decent place to live in, it's a big pity if their husbands can't even stand to be around—just looking on, of course, not helping.

And so it goes. For some obscure reason, women keep on doing it. I have a strong suspicion that in a large percentage of cases it's just a habit: Grandma and Mamma cleaned house spring and fall, so they do too. They are in an old rut and don't go to the trouble of thinking up a nice new one of their own. I can only wonder whether a woman who feels that twice a year the whole house has simply got to be perfectly clean all at once doesn't suffer acutely when it begins to get progressively dirtier. How can she stand that? The pleasant sensation one gets from thinking of how clean things are isn't foreign to me, but I'm not greedy; I can feel quite virtuous about just one closet, or even one shelf in one closet.

I can imagine but one sensible reason for such whirlwind tactics. We all know that every now and then brass has to be polished, pictures must be washed, walls wiped down, and so forth (the extent of the "so forth" depending on how much stuff demanding attention you keep around). I can understand the housekeeper who hates this extra-special cleaning but knows it must be done and prefers to ruin herself twice a year and get the suffering all over with at once than do it piecemeal. A drastic solution.

Suppose that instead of calling it spring and fall cleaning, we name it basic cleaning, for by my method there's no season for it and no schedule. I may perhaps give it fifteen minutes or half an hour right after lunch, or omit it if I want to or, if I'm in the mood, stay with it for an hour or two. Taking down pictures and washing them, doing windows, closets, pantry shelves and dresser drawers, polishing brass and any number of other jobs can be done for only fifteen minutes at one time, and in that way you don't notice the energy and time they consume. Actually, I don't think there's anything in this category of basic cleaning that demands that I stay at it after I've had enough. And you can be just as methodical, or not, as your inclination suggests: finish one room before you start another, or be completely haphazard. The condition something is in may influence you; for example, if a drawer or shelf is beginning to drive you crazy because of its untidiness, perhaps you had better put it in order.

If I am waiting for a telephone call before going out to the garden, I may wash a picture or two. One day you may decide to clean the top pantry shelf, and before you know it you're interested and full of vigor and you do the whole pantry. You may have worked a few hours instead of the few minutes you had planned on, but you enjoyed it because you did it when you felt like it, and not because you had to. That should appeal to you who hate basic housecleaning. Eventually everything gets the treatment, but you hardly know how or when it happened. And if something you don't notice gets overlooked by this happy-go-lucky method, what, pray, is the difference? You won't be exhausted so you won't get cranky, and when Mother is irritable everyone around suffers. The children are likely to be scolded and punished unfairly, while Father is pretty much cowed, and all feel guilty; Mother is a wreck and in some vague way it seems to be their fault.

To those of you who like having the whole house spotless at one time, I want to emphasize that by your system you can have this pleasure only twice a year, and then for only a fleeting period. But by my method you can have, over and over through the fifty-two weeks, the pleasure of thinking, such-and-such is fresh and clean and it was no trouble at all.

You may think that's rather piddling. Well, the world is full and running over with pleasant and unpleasant trifles. If you never again in your life have the satisfaction of knowing that your whole house is immaculate at one time, you can very easily substitute some other delightful thoughts. In spring you can dwell on trees and shrubs coming to life again, on the new hat you just bought, and vacation time approaching. In the fall you can look forward to gleaming snow and cozy privacy in the country or theatre and music in the city. And isn't it splendid that you're not too irritable and worn out from drastic house-cleaning to enjoy these things?

Although destiny may cripple us, take away the one we love best, deny us our dearest wish, we can still, unless we are just too mixed up in our thinking, make a determined effort to slam the door in the face of depressing thoughts. If the pantry shelves are clean and the kitchen ones aren't, think of those in the pantry, for goodness' sake.

There are many difficulties which other people present to us, but there are also quite a few which we bring on ourselves. The latter are much easier to control; only two things are necessary. The first is to be quite sure that, everything considered, we want to make a change, and the second is to go ahead and make it.

VIII

Turning Pennies into Dollars

Although in most homes today men are still the providers and women the spenders, there has been quite a change in the actual handling of the pay envelope. It used to be that the housewife—who usually worked as long and as hard as her husband—seldom had a nickel to call her own. If the children needed shoes or if she needed stockings, she had to ask for the money, often explain what it was for, argue that it was essential, and now and then she would fail to get it. There has been quite a departure from that routine, but there's no fixed rule. Sometimes the wage earner gives his wife only a certain amount for running the house; others add to this a sum for her personal use, still others give her the whole paycheck, keeping only enough for their own weekly expenses and letting her manage the finances.

When people get married they are, let us hope, very much in love, and to make even one aspect of their future life together sound like a business deal is probably at this point repugnant to them. The question is, just when does it no longer seem obnoxious? One definite, business-like discussion, no matter how romantic you may feel about each other, seems to me more desirable than wrangling or hurt feelings or an unjust arrangement, any of which may follow a lack of understanding at the outset.

If a marriage ends in divorce, the wife who has held up her end at home while her husband earned the money may face a rough time if the "breadwinner" has had control of all his earnings. Or it may be the man who is hit the hardest; a woman whose only occupation is sitting around being an ex-wife while collecting money from her former husband, whether he can afford it or not, must have to do an expert job of rationalizing in order to hang on to her self-respect.

But even in successful marriages, the handling of money can be a constant bone of contention. If a girl had never earned any money before she married, if she had had to go to her parents every time she wanted anything from an ice cream soda to a new coat, she might be reasonably contented if she married a man who felt he had the right to say with some authority, "That's too much to pay for a dress." But if she ever had a job she is likely to expect to have a dollar now and then for her very own, to spend foolishly from the husband's point of view without its being any of his business.

Recently I had a letter from a woman somewhere in the Midwest, ordering an autographed copy of my book about gardening and going into detail about her vegetables and flowers. She said that her favorite flower was the peony but she had only one bush because her husband was crazy about tulips, and they couldn't afford all they wanted of each. As I read on I learned that her husband had, in fact, eight hundred tulip bulbs and was aiming for a thousand.

In some households that sort of thing could create a situation. However, this woman's letter was pleasant and uncomplaining. It was obvious that much as she longed for more peonies, she wanted still more for her husband to have a thousand tulips. I decided that she must be really devoted to his happiness, for she had apparently never let him know her preference. Or perhaps she was just clever, realizing that even if he did know he might still make a stand for more tulips, and then she might resent his selfishness.

Not many of us can give up our personal likes and wishes and be contented and cheerful about it year after year. The safest thing is to guard our own interests in as reasonable and cheerful a manner as possible so that, if for no better reason, we won't become sour and feel put upon. For myself I know that I would rather have a dollar a week to do with as I please than a generous handing-out of larger bills accompanied by good advice about how to spend them. And I should think that a man, parting with the money he has perhaps earned by hard work at something he doesn't like, could hardly bear it if his wife spends it for things that he thinks are nonsense. Actually I don't know of anyone who thoroughly approves of the way anybody else saves or spends his money. We're even irritated when it in no way affects us. How much worse it must feel when the money being "squandered" came from the toil of our own hands or brains!

Fred and I started our life together with a definite money arrangement, never mind that there was almost none to arrange; anyway, it kept us from having financial arguments. It's simple; he gives me a small sum each week, I do the work, and he pays all expenses except my personal ones. Which reminds me of a little incident of some years ago which I look back on now with considerable amazement. Fred sold a small piece of property and offered me fifty dollars with the provision that I spend it at once for something for myself. But when I was about thirty-five years old, I had suddenly realized one day that I was using a shocking percentage of my waking hours doing nothing more interesting or imaginative than making money, and I had at once found myself a part-time job, thus exchanging money for time. From then on I had through the years cut down my desire for material possessions to the lowest minimum anyone could believe and so, try as I did that day, I couldn't think of a single thing I wanted, and I didn't get the money. Such lack of ingenuity! I wouldn't be caught that way again although, to tell the truth, I can't think of anything I want today either. But by golly, I'll put my mind to it and come up with *something* if I ever get another such offer.

Now let's have a look at the family budget. Shall we start with those two menaces, the charge account and installment buying? The former should be indulged in only, it seems to me, by those who don't have to care how fast the money is flying out the window. And installment buying is primarily for those who want something, haven't the money to pay cash, and can't wait until they have. However, their inability to wait may not be an actual need for the product, such as having to buy a car in order to get to work; it may be a psychological condition in which an adequate car must be replaced by a new one because the latest models are so tempting and, besides, what will people *think!*

Do you realize that when you pay cash at a store that carries charge accounts you pay more for what you buy because others prefer not to pay as they go? A store charges for its products at a rate which brings in a certain profit, and in figuring what to charge for goods they must take into consideration many factors. Carrying charge accounts means that they have to wait for their money; they also sustain losses from being unable to collect a certain percentage of what is owed. And handling these accounts involves extra time and expense for bookkeeping, follow-up letters and so on. This is taken into consideration every time an item of goods is priced for sale, so when you pay cash you are charged more than you would need to be if some people didn't want the convenience of a charge account.

Buying on the installment plan is another thing entirely. The person who gets the "benefit" of this way of buying is the one who pays through the nose; he is charged more for the item than the cash customers are.

There is some kind of subtle, perhaps unrecognized snobbishness in the distinction between these two types of buying. A person who is permitted to open a charge account has to be one who can be expected to pay his bills, while anyone who buys an article on the installment plan is a person who presumably hasn't enough cash to pay for it. Therefore, if this feeling of superiority is actually present, if I am not just imagining it, then it boils down to the unfortunately prevalent feeling that a person who has money is superior to one who hasn't. But I guess we didn't have to go through all that to know that this point of view abounds.

People brought up with money are completely blind to the biggest problem the majority of humans face, which is the job of somehow getting enough to eat in order to stay alive, and of getting a stove to cook it on, and a chair to sit on while they eat it and a bed to rest on so that they can conserve their energy and be able to join the daily struggle for bread again tomorrow. I know a wealthy, kindly woman, with ideals so lofty that they are sometimes over my head (and I'm no slouch at thinking up lofty ideals), but she forgets to pay the men who work for her, and they have to ask for it several times before they get their money. Hard as it may be to believe, this woman is really well-meaning, just completely unrealistic. One day, during the last war she stopped in when I was canning vegetables, and as we chatted I remarked that because of food rationing a friend of mine in New York had persuaded me to sell her some of my canned produce. My caller asked if she, too, could buy some and, picking up a quart jar of corn, asked how much I charged for it.

I told her and she thought it was expensive. How had I arrived at the price? I explained: so much for the jar, the corn, the electricity, the labor.

"Oh well, if you're going to charge for your labor!" she exclaimed.

Now, if my opinion of charge accounts and installment buying hasn't leaked through, I'll put it in one sentence: I think both of those ways of buying are excellent things to avoid, and I'll add a piece of information. Recently a man who works in a jewelry store told us that the policy there was to sell on the installment plan but not to charge anything extra for goods sold this way, because the boss *preferred* installment buyers. Every time the customer came in to make the monthly payment he (usually she) was likely to be tempted by another piece and would begin making payments on it too. I don't know how that strikes you, but it makes me feel that I would just as soon not be *tricked* into spending my money.

There's more than one reason for being economical. One is simply a hatred of waste; another is the need (real or imagined) to be careful in your spending for fear you'll land on relief. There is also a sort of one-sided economy: saving on one type of thing so that you will have more to spend on something else. And there is of course the reason about which there can be no ifs nor buts: the money just isn't there to spend.

I am impatient of waste, perhaps unduly. It seems to me there's a certain arrogance in it, including the waste in nature. In fact, I abhor it to such an extent that if, for instance, I was staying in a hotel and for some reason got so mad at the management that I hoped they would go bankrupt, I think I still would turn off all lights if I went out for the evening.

The second type of economist I spoke of I am not. It's true that the older I grow the more inclined I am to wonder sometimes if what we have will see us through to the end, but I am constitutionally unable to give this much thought. All my life I have had enough to eat, a reasonably comfortable bed and good health, which is perhaps more than my share. If I should have to end my life in the poorhouse, I might find the experience interesting and even instructive, who knows?

But I do belong in that third category; I can cheerfully do without ninety-nine things in order to be able to buy the hundredth. Maybe I'm just snooty; I can get along very well without items that cost only a dime or a quarter or even a dollar. There's truth in that axiom about taking care of the dimes (or is it pennies?) and the dollars will take care of themselves. I learned this when I was very young; with no dollars to worry about, I saved pennies and lo! dollars showed up!

Of course it would be rather grim to go through life constantly wanting to squander a little money and having to remind yourself each time not to. But it's quite possible, for some temperaments, to reach an attitude whereby you hardly ever want to buy needlessly and, having achieved this, you may surprisingly soon have a nice sum to be crazy reckless with if you wish. Or to put in the bank if that suits you better.

I don't know what distinction the dictionary makes between the words "stingy" and "economical"; to me a stingy person is one who tries to get away without paying his share, while an economical one tries to figure out ways of saving money on various things in order to buy himself, or others, either security or some commodity which he values more than the one he denies himself. The stingy person is unlovely; the economical one is to my mind both sensible and discriminating.

The unfortunate part about the kind of economies I am now about to suggest is that you can have no way of knowing at any given time how much they have earned for you. At no point can you say, I'm so-and-so much richer because I did this and that. Therefore, why bother? Well, if it seems like a bother and is painful to you, I would say you're better off to skip it. But if waste is distasteful to you, or if you're having a tough time making the grade financially, or if it annoys you somewhat to spend twenty-five cents when twenty would answer the same purpose, there are quite a few little economies that are no trouble at all, once you put them into practice. And some of them automatically save you time as well as money.

First of all, let's not be ashamed of bothering to save the pennies. Waxed paper is quite a bit more expensive than butcher paper, which answers the same purpose; if you have room to store it, buy a whole roll of butcher paper. It will last for ages. It's a big bulky unwieldy thing, so take an empty waxed-paper box and roll off onto the cardboard cylinder a good supply of the butcher paper. Put it into the waxed-paper box, and it's as handy as you could wish. Also, the paper that bread comes wrapped in is satisfactory in size, shape, and quality for keeping left-overs to be put into the refrigerator. The cost: zero.

If you cook with electricity, it's quite surprising the amount of current you can save. Or waste. If you believe, as I do, that most vegetables should be cooked only until they are fairly tender (for the sake of both flavor and vitamins), you will find that many need only be brought to a brisk boil and then will finish on the hot burner with the current turned off. And except for beets, almost any other two vegetables (or even three) may be warmed over in the same vessel. They will soon be getting along nicely together on your plate, why not in a pot? This saves not only electricity but washing. Moreover, as you know, time and current are used up just getting a burner hot. It is therefore practical sometimes to use one burner for two different pots, and if this sounds clumsy here's one example. Say you are having soup and a left-over vegetable for lunch; when the soup has become hot enough, remove it, put the vegetable on the hot burner, and almost before you've served the soup, the vegetable will be heated. You can also save electricity—and time—by taking the food out of the refrigerator for awhile before it's to be heated.

When using the oven for the main dish, you can often manage to cook the entire meal in it, although this doesn't seem worth while if it's much extra trouble. But sometimes it works out nicely: if I am baking biscuits for breakfast and we're also having ham and eggs, I put the ham in a skillet, break the eggs around the meat, and cook the concoction in the oven. If you time it perfectly, the ham and eggs taste better, we think, than when cooked on top of the stove.

I never try to save on light in the kitchen. We have a fluorescent one in the middle of the ceiling and additional lights over the sink and stove. In the saving of both time and money, one thing to keep in mind is that the idea of the whole business is to make things, in some way or other, better for you, and working without proper light isn't sensible.

Here's a small item, yet it may save enough in a year to buy a pair of earrings, or a bottle of sherry. When I start to wash dishes, the first thing I do is to let the water run off until it's very hot, and if I have any plants (indoors or out) which could use some, I catch what I run off and give it to them. It's warm, but we are told that plants are better off with warm water. If nothing more, this has the advantage of making you take care of this job at a regular time, and for all we know plants thrive under a regular routine just as the human body is said to do.

There is some kind of a feud between me and grease; I hate to get my hands greasy and I hate to put greasy spoons, pans and so on into clean water. Now there's no softer paper, except tissue and paper napkins, than the telephone book. Not only that, the pages are exactly the right size for various purposes. I keep an old one handy and when my fingers get greasy, I grab a page and wipe them. And before I wash any greasy cup, spoon, or pan, it gets a thorough wiping with a few more pages. Cost: zero. There is more to it than that; many years ago a plumber told me that if women didn't put greasy dishes and pots in the sink, and if they would finish every job of dishwashing with clean, hot, soapy water, they would never have to call a plumber because the pipes were clogged.

A while back I came across a suggestion that toilet paper be used in the kitchen instead of paper towels because it's cheaper. I never had the courage to do that; I wouldn't mind the association myself but I know I couldn't endure the boredom of having to laugh politely at all the remarks (or rather, the same one with slight variations) which would be forthcoming. I'll stick to the telephone book.

If you have space for it, it's always wise to buy in large quantities. Speaking of being petty, have you ever noticed that items in bulk, such as cheese, are always priced at odd figures? Something at sixty cents a pound would mean that a half pound would be thirty cents. That would do the merchant no good, but if he prices it at sixty-one cents, when you buy half a pound you will pay thirty-one cents. Two people buy a half pound each and the merchant gets sixty-two cents for his pound instead of sixty-one. Big Business isn't ashamed to use its head to make a penny, why should you be?

In all cases, it pays to buy in quantity if you can. If there's something you use fairly constantly—say canned tomatoes—you might be surprised at how much you will save if you buy them by the case. Also, watch for sales and stock up. Merchants often sell something at a loss just to get you in the store, did you know that? For a good many people the trouble with buying by the case is that they don't have the money "this week." If you are more or less one of these, living from hand to mouth, it's one of the few instances in which I think you would be wise to borrow some money to avail yourself of a good buy.

And then a respectful attitude toward left-overs won't hurt the budget a bit. Even if you haven't a freezer or ice-chamber, you needn't throw out good food; every vegetable is good served cold with a bit of dressing on it—French, mayonnaise, sour cream. One combination we especially like is horseradish, mayonnaise and sour cream. You can either put a little dressing on last night's vegetable and serve it for lunch, or you can save all left-over vegetables for a few days, then mix them together with some dressing and serve them for dinner. You may be surprised at how popular this will be with the family.

As you no doubt know, left-over potatoes of almost any kind are very good fried. I often scramble them with two or three eggs for our lunch; dried onion added to this gives a nice flavor. I make a few patties with the left-over mashed potatoes, browning them on both sides. Or the mashed potatoes can be added to gravy to thicken it. Or put into soup.

Small amounts of left-over meat make a very good soup just by adding water and bouillon cubes or soup stock; a few days of bits of such meat will make soup for the whole family. Somewhat larger amounts, which are still not enough for another meal, may be saved and combined with other remnants later; these can be labeled and will take up only a little space in the freezer compartment.

When a small family has a too-large roast and no freezer, they are usually faced with the necessity of eating the remainder more often than they might like. But most of the curse can be taken off this one way or another. If you adopt the method of slow roasting, you can buy the smallest roast possible, for it won't dry out in the cooking. With a left-over veal or lamb roast, for instance, you can have a curry; just add a *good* brand of curry powder to the gravy. If your family doesn't go for curried meat, try adding a can of mushrooms instead. And speaking of economy, when you buy canned mushrooms for casseroles, stews, and the like, you will save if you get the "stems and pieces" instead of the whole or sliced mushrooms. They taste exactly the same, of course. Similarly, there are a number of people around who don't know that you can buy cracked eggs and they'll be considerably cheaper. You can't boil them, but you can do plenty of other things with them. I don't believe that it's widely known, either, that broken cookies and crackers can be bought quite inexpensively.

If everybody were obliged to buy cracked eggs and broken crackers, that would be one thing, but a situation in which some people don't even know such things exist while others, in the effort to make ends meet, feel they must buy them, disturbs me. There's surely something out of kilter in a world in which some people are so poor that if others, more fortunate, were to hear the details of that poverty, it would make them feel they were being told of another species of animal. Something like finding out that earthworms can be cut in two and go on living.

That little outburst is for the benefit of you who are forced to economize. If you can come through the piddling penny-savings without resenting them excessively, and without putting an inflated value on all the little and big luxuries that money could give you, you will, in the long run, be a more complete person, with fuller understanding of your fellow creatures, than the woman who can offhandedly use up a pint of cream, a pound of butter, a dozen eggs in preparing a meal. You will probably also be more efficient and resourceful, and may be spared agonizing over your weight.

For the rest of you, if you're dying for a bit of advice, here it is: if you don't *have* to be saving, try not to run your passion for economy into the ground; don't let it rule you. On the other hand, don't be ashamed of it; if you like to practice certain little economies, don't mind what anyone else may think of them. There's a vast difference between stinginess and a dislike of waste. Take the matter of lights being turned on throughout the house, even though they're not needed. We know a few families who do this, yet insist they can't buy food by the case because they don't have the money. These people, I would say, are unintelligently wasteful. (Come to think of it, is there such a thing as intelligent squandering?) On the other hand, I met a woman recently who remarked, "I wish I could reform, but I don't seem to be able to. I keep my house blazing with lights every night because somehow it gives me such a wonderful feeling."

"Well, that may be an extravagant habit," I replied, "but in my opinion it isn't wasteful. Anything that gives you a sense of pleasure isn't a waste."

Nor is it a waste, I think, to spend money "foolishly" if it irritates you to watch it carefully. It seems, though, that some people consider it niggardly to try to save on the electric bill, and how this idea got started I can't imagine. It wouldn't make sense, would it, if you went into someone's kitchen and found the water running and your hostess said, "I left it on. It seems so stingy to turn it off just because I'm not using it."

In general, it seems to me that the most interesting way to save anything, whether it's time or money or energy, is to think of it in terms of the more desirable thing you are going to do with it. There's a story about a Chinese and a New Yorker who were waiting together on the platform for a subway train at rush hour, and the Chinese asked why people shoved and pushed and struggled to get into the express trains when the locals were relatively empty. The New Yorker replied that you saved a certain number of minutes if you took an express.

"So? And what do the people do with those minutes they save?" inquired the Chinese.

Of course the point in saving money is to be able to use it for something you need or enjoy more than, for example, that wasted electricity. But the whole thing will seem meaningless to you if you consider it in terms of any particular isolated instance; it's your over-all attitude that counts, something like a clock which bothers with only one second at a time but inevitably gets there.

However, it's important to keep your balance; I've been told so often that I'm an extremist that I'm beginning to believe it. I know I'm somewhat inclined to be over-impressed with my cleverness in budgeting, and perhaps I go too far, sometimes serving unnecessarily humble meals just for the satisfaction of being able to admire my resourcefulness. Lately, though, I've been trying to reform, asking myself, is it worth while to give so much thought to the saving of a little money, even though I might be able at the same time to admire my ingenuity? I have also learned that Fred would be pleased to have lobster served oftener, never mind the cost. Another thing: which is more valuable, one's time and strength, or money? If I've already done enough work today and expensive canapés are easier to fix, we have them. This new attitude of mine may force us to sell the old homestead, since I *am* inclined to go to extremes. In the meantime, though, while the mood lasts, let's get out the steak knives a little oftener.

In the process of acquiring something for your own either "sensible" or "frivolous" enjoyment, I hope you'll go merrily on your way, taking heed only that you're not hurting anyone. That is, if you're skimping on meals in order to buy yourself a bracelet, or if you're quickly tossing together inferior dishes so that you may spend more time playing bridge or writing poetry, perhaps somebody may have the right to growl at you. But if you are fulfilling your obligations, keeping up your end, let no one intimidate you. Very few of us have so much time and money with which to do exactly as we please that we can afford to squander it; far too much of both is spent in keeping in step with those miserable Joneses, whom someone should have done away with long ago.

IX

Making Time for Yourself

Many women constantly complain that they have no time for themselves. Before we start giving aid and comfort to them, let's for a moment consider those who do have some time on their hands, for oddly enough some of the same problems apply. For one thing, have you ever stopped to ask yourself why you want more leisure? Or what you would do with it if you had it? In fact, what *do* you do with what you have? We can't be miserly with time, can't hoard the hours we save each day; we must spend them at once, and many women seem to make a botch of this, not from my point of view but from their own.

There are, for instance, the elderly women who live alone, those with security, fairly good health and a few friends. They are under obligation to no one. Their time is their own, but unfortunately this often seems to be just another burden they have to bear. Old men are in even a worse fix; it's more difficult for them to think up little jobs to do at home, and one sees them standing around on street corners, watching the people go by. If you are lonely, yet are unable to find a way to get close to a single one of the many human beings around you—well, that must be pretty grim.

Now what about that lucky woman who has her family around her but whose children are at last old enough to allow her that longed-for freedom? She's as busy as ever, but now it's with various projects which conflict and overlap, and she's still complaining that she has no time of her own for doing as she pleases. However, she can no longer blame her over-full life on anyone but herself.

Webster calls leisure "time at one's command, *free from engagement; period of unengaged time; ease.*" (Italics mine.) A leisure hour, then, seems to be one in which we can do exactly as we please, and it sounds like Paradise to anyone who feels driven. But one look at the many lonely old men and women, at the restless people who have retired, at the full-to-overflowing hours of the very woman who could hardly wait to be free from the turmoil of her child-rearing days is enough to convince us that leisure that we haven't learned how to enjoy is something to be avoided if possible. Once again man's ingenuity is out of step with his ability to make his inventiveness serve him to the best purpose. In some ways he uses his mind to almost startling advantage, while in others he doesn't seem to use it at all.

For you who are truly longing for a little free time, I have some simple suggestions. You will think up many of your own if you put your mind to it. Meanwhile, let's begin in the kitchen, which takes up a large share of most women's waking hours. Some modern kitchens I've seen remind me of the office desks of important executives: nothing in sight to indicate that any work is ever done around there. If you're crowded for kitchen space, I suppose you're obliged to put things out of the way, but if you can swing it, I suggest you try leaving some of your working tools out handy.

On the wall by the stove in my own kitchen is a wooden rack which Fred made to hold every knife, fork, spoon, scissors which I need in cooking. Low nails and hooks between the stove and the wall hold pancake turner, potato masher, potholders and skillets, which are all out of sight. On the rack is a pair of pliers and a screwdriver. What are these used for? Oh a number of things; for instance, the pliers quickly pull the rubber ring out of a jar of canned tomatoes; the screwdriver will help to open the can of baking powder, curry, etc. Near the stove is the wall can opener, and close by is the bottle and jar opener, a gadget I would be sunk without. At the right of the stove in a large shallow drawer in the workbench are salt, pepper, garlic squeezer, meat thermometer, onion and spiced salt seasonings.

There are two long shelves over the stove; on the lower one I keep casserole dishes, a pewter coffeepot and an old-fashioned coffee grinder which we use when the electric one breaks down. The upper shelf is dedicated entirely to beauty; it is filled with old china, most of which belonged to my two grandmothers.

A few of the pieces were in Fred's family. For one reason or another most of them aren't practical for daily use, but I like to have them where we and others can enjoy them.

However, the shelf containing this china is directly over the stove, so the pieces get more than merely dusty; they collect a sort of greasy film. So, with a life overflowing with things I love to do, and others I'm obliged to do, the problem is to keep the china clean without making a burden of it. Happily, I've thought of a way: almost every day when I'm doing the lunch dishes, I also wash one or two of the old pieces, wipe off that part of the shelf where they stand, and put them back. I skip only the days when we have company for lunch, or when I'm in a hurry or am merely disinclined. And although in the long run I've used as much time as I would have if I had washed them all at once, the job hasn't cut into anything else I may have wanted to do. This is like giving someone a penny each day in the year; you wouldn't miss it, but if you were asked for an outright gift of $3.65 you might be unwilling to part with it.

It is extremely handy to keep your flour, sugar, onions, potatoes in bins; mine are in the drawers of the kitchen workbench which Fred made. I hope that those of you who don't have such a convenient arrangement have thought up something easier than taking down a container from shelf or closet every time you need a little flour or sugar.

Almost everyone seems to be wedded to his or her particular way of washing dishes. Some do them under running hot water, others like to stop up the sink and use it for a dishpan. Some wipe; others drain. I consider my system superior in every way to all others, and I doubt if anyone could persuade me even to try his; I'm just as closed-minded about this issue as the next one. But I'm not going to describe my way; I have yet to see anyone change his politics, religion, or method of washing dishes just because somebody has better to offer.

One way of saving time is obvious, yet I've known intelligent women who don't take advantage of it, so I'll mention it. There are jobs such as browning meat for a pot roast or stew, or making applesauce, or cooking pumpkin or winter squash, which require your presence but don't demand your constant attention. Instead of just waiting around, start them when you are about to do the dishes, or get a window or two washed, or how about polishing some silver?

Does this sound hectic? Are you thinking, "Good heavens, why doesn't she just sit down and rest a few minutes while something cooks?" If that appeals to you, fine. But although I'm something of an expert at resting, I'm not good at it with a job on my mind; I prefer to concentrate wholly on work, then play. However, ignore my splendid suggestions if you like a mixture of the two; you'll be better off following your own inclinations.

A good deal of time can be saved in marketing if we give it some thought. Of course you keep a handy pad in the kitchen to jot down items you need. I buy several packages at a time of all staples such as rice, beans, crackers, and so on; when I open the next-to-last box of anything, that item goes on the pad. This is a good way to avoid running out of any commodity —and to save shopping time.

This is the gadget era; housewives live in fairyland: press a button, flip a switch, turn a faucet. If our grandmothers could have believed the forecast of all the labor-saving devices, no doubt they would have gasped, "What on earth will women do with all that free time?" They themselves, perhaps, would have made more quilts.

I'm afraid that most young mothers today, except perhaps those living in the city, would answer Grandma's question by snapping, "*What* free time?" For it seems that the handy automobile has presented them with quite a job; all the ingenuity of man, and his eagerness to help out and his willingness to profit financially by producing one gadget after another, haven't so far figured out a way (since walking has gone out of style) for children to get to dancing class, swimming pool, kindergarten, parties, other than by having Mother take them in the car. If you don't understand how this situation can make life hectic for a mother, ask one who has several children. These women admittedly live in turmoil and are outspokenly sorry for themselves. If only they had a little time to do as they pleased, preferably nothing!

I'm devoted to a few gadgets that are convenient rather than time-saving, though saving energy and strain are almost the same thing, at least as far as one's sense of well-being is concerned. Anyhow, one is a tin contraption to hold paper bags. The holder is fastened to the wall. Haven't you found it maddening to have a lot of paper bags around in such disorder that you never can find the size you want? Another is a timer which I can use to call me from couch and book, ordering me to the kitchen, but leaving me and my mind free until it does.

The king of gadgets, in my opinion, is the home freezer. A big one, by all means. However, when we were buying our first one some eleven or twelve years ago, I was just short of aghast when Fred casually bought one with a capacity of seven hundred pounds. The man who sold it to us said we should keep it full in order to hold down the expense of running it. Full of *what!* Fred and I were then in our early sixties, and I told myself that if by some magic we did eventually get that immense vacuum filled up with food we couldn't possibly live long enough to use it up, even though, by heredity, we both have long life expectancies.

On the way home we discussed at great length where we would put the white elephant, which was my tactfully unspoken name for the object. Our kitchen is large, but the walls are taken up with a stove, a sink, long workbench, three doors and two cupboards. Obviously no room for it there. The pantry would hold it if we took down some shelves and moved the big old refrigerator into the little back entrance hall and, for my money, this was the place for it.

Tentatively, Fred mentioned the cellar. I knew that this was where many people had their freezers, and I suppose they get used to it, the way they would to having only one leg, but I couldn't have been more against anything. It's true that I wasn't sure that I would ever be able to think up much of anything to put in the freezer, but in case I did I definitely wasn't in favor of having to take a trip down the steep cellar stairs in order to do it.

Three men arrived with the huge, bulky thing and looked the situation over. The cellar was at once ruled out; it would be quite impossible, they said, to get the freezer down there without tearing most of the house down. They were also very much against the pantry; too much work involved. For them, that is.

They did their utmost to persuade us that the garage was the ideal place. Now, that building is sixty feet from the back door and downhill, a perfect spot to get to on an icy day, in the middle of winter, after dark, if I should happen to want a package of peas for dinner.

Fred said No. They tried to argue. Finally I chipped in, "Do you want death from pneumonia on your conscience, or a mess of broken bones? Look at my white hair, for pity's sake!"

Well, I doubt if they gave a darn about how many bones I might break, but they were keen enough to see that we were stubborn, so they gave in. The pantry was decided on.

They had to do things to the narrow door, take out a window, and so on, but finally, to my complete amazement, that immense thing was actually sitting in our pantry and taking up at least half its space.

I don't remember now what I was told to do before we turned on the power, but I did it. Then you're supposed to get the box plenty cold and fill it to the top.

Fill it? Seven hundred pounds? With what, pray?

In writing a friend in New York I had mentioned our new toy, and when she and her husband drove out that weekend, they brought the freezer a present, a quart of ice-cream. We christened the baby with it, placing it down on the bottom of the box, and I've never seen anything look so forlorn, so lonely, so ridiculous as that small package in that abyss. Obviously, something should be added at once to keep it company, but I was waiting for an inspiration; so far none had shown up.

You may think this all sounds somewhat stupid, and no doubt it was. But several intelligent women I know have had freezers for years and don't even yet begin to make the most of them. One of them said to me not long ago, "I can't think of a thing to put in our freezer except bread."

Eventually I got around to reading carefully the instruction book which came with the object, and immediately began to freeze whatever vegetables in our garden were ready to pick (this was August). Then I went on to bushels of peaches, various meats, some local chickens, and by late autumn I was wishing for more freezer space. This could have been embarrassing, for I had glibly told several friends that we had loads of freezer room, would they care to put in a few turkeys, and so forth? Luckily they all were slow to take advantage of my offer, so no situations arose.

Is a freezer economical? Does it actually save you money? When I began to realize what having one was doing for me in the realm of making my life easier, when I began to say sincerely to my friends, "I think I'd almost rather do without running water than a freezer," that was the first question asked. And always the next remark was, "It's all right for people like you who have a garden and freeze vegetables for the winter, but otherwise I can't see much point in it."

In the beginning I didn't know what to reply. Taking into account the original investment, the cost of a repair man once in a while, and the electricity used, it seemed to me that you would have to use a freezer quite a long time before it could be considered a money-saving proposition, even if you did freeze your own produce. So I would stammer and stutter and try, without success, to transfer a little of my enthusiasm.

Then one day the obvious answer came to me: why does a freezer have to be economical? Does your electric dishwasher, two-oven stove, or television or vacuum cleaner save you money? A freezer, like all those other things, isn't supposed to do that, but it does clutter up your life with leisure, and if you can't think of anything to do with those invaluable hours, maybe a freezer isn't for you.

One big thing about having a freezer is the time you save in shopping; since we've had one, I doubt if we've made as many as three trips a year to town just for the purpose of buying food. We keep the freezer stocked with all kinds of meat, fish, bread, rolls, butter, orange juice, vegetables, several kinds of fruit, raw tomato juice, cheese. When Fred has to go to Danbury for one reason or another, he replenishes any of the items that are running low. Then, too, you can prepare a number of things in advance and save a lot of time in preparation later, when you may not be in the mood.

So here we are with a freezer full of meats, vegetables, desserts; a lot of dinners are practically ready. And now I'll try to answer the question that I should think would be in some of your minds: how on earth do I figure that I've saved so much time when I've spent hours making stews, pot roasts, freezing vegetables and fruits, and on and on?

Look at it this way. The work in browning meat for stew and the other beef dishes is the longest job and takes me roughly two hours; I get from this twenty-odd meals. This means that it takes me six minutes to prepare the meat for dinner. If you want to be picayune about it, you can add on a few minutes for putting in some vegetables, or paprika and sour cream, or whatever you're going to doll the dish up with. It takes even less time to prepare lamb shanks, pot roasts, short ribs. A big turkey provides from fifteen to twenty freezer meals, and unless you're going to make a cream sauce for it, there's no work involved beyond opening the freezer door and helping yourself.

If you stock up an assortment of commercially frozen vegetables, obviously the least time possible is spent on them. If you prefer to use "fresh" vegetables during the winter, you must spend time shopping for and preparing them. If you freeze your own home-grown vegetables it takes time but, for many of them, much less than you would imagine until you've tried it.

Whether or not you save time on desserts depends entirely on what you would serve if your freezer wasn't well-stocked with frozen fruits. You can figure that out for yourself.

There's no question that you can save many hours in preparing meals if you have a freezer and use your brain. However, for me it has a value beyond that: the great thing is that I can do almost all of my cooking when I feel like it instead of being driven to the kitchen an hour or two before dinner every day in the week.

Many years ago my sister-in-law said to me that she didn't mind cooking as much as she did having to decide what to serve. I wasn't a housewife in those days, and that sounded far-fetched to me. When, later, I was faced with thinking up daily menus, I was inclined to agree with her. I have the feeling that the meal is half ready if I know what I'm going to have. With a variety of meats, vegetables, desserts on hand, awaiting my pleasure, I like to jot down a week's menus in advance. Subject to change, of course. So the only problem remaining is how to locate just what you're looking for in that well-stocked storehouse, and that can be a difficult one, I admit.

Why do I end this long tribute to the inestimable values of a freezer in a minor key? It's not really so minor, though. Wouldn't it be unreasonable to expect to open the door—any door—reach in and take out exactly what you want? Does anybody or anything in this world always give you exactly what you want at just the moment when you want it?

If a freezer is a boon to womankind, there's another gadget, the telephone, which is, to say the least, a mixed blessing. But we can stop being a slave to it, rather than just complaining about it, as I've heard so many women do. If you're against leaving the receiver off the hook now and then when you're fed up, you can ignore it when it rings; many people can't bear to do this, but with a little practice it's easy. And with the dial system you can think up some handy signals. One of my friends dials my number and hangs up after two rings, and another friend after three rings, and I do the same for them. Then we call each other back when it's convenient. You can also earn a lot of gratitude if you will find out which hours various people prefer not to be disturbed.

But why, instead of my sitting here overworking my brain trying to think up some more bad habits for you to avoid because they're nothing but time consumers, and good habits to adopt because they will save you time, don't I suggest that you have for yourself a time-saving week, beginning now? All day long watch yourself perform, and figure out improvements. The object in view is to earn some leisure and then protect it.

In today's world, when news can come that a friend living thousands of miles away is planning to drop in on us tomorrow, not counting all the ones who live nearby, it's vital to learn to say No if we're to decide for ourselves how we are going to spend our time. It needn't be very difficult to explain to your friends that you value your hours and have definite plans for them. Nobody is going to ask you for, or snatch out of your hand, the money that you expect to use to buy yourself a dress, even though he may think you don't need one. Why should he then be hurt if you want your own hour or your own day to do with as you please? You can say No without being blunt or rude about it, most people will understand if you explain how you feel, and if you think it will help, you can call yourself "odd" before they have a chance to. Anyhow, if you aren't really attached to a person, does it matter if he's annoyed at your attitude? And if you are fond of someone, surely you can make him realize it and hold his affection without being obliged to buy it with either your money or your time.

X

For Better—We Hope

RECENTLY I attended a wedding. The bride was glowing. I don't know about a groom, but I believe that every young bride, if she's marrying for love, feels that the thrill and romance will last forever, despite the less-than-inspiring marriages she has probably observed. The word "obey" had been deleted from the ceremony, which seems to me a step forward, but "love" and "honor" remained. I remember when women began to make a stand against promising to obey a husband; good for them, I thought, but I didn't understand (and I still don't) why they were willing to promise to love and honor a man for the rest of their lives. You can at least keep a vow to obey, if you want to, but no amount of determination and will power and good faith will help you to continue to love and honor anyone; that takes other ingredients which may be out of your power, or the other person's, to supply. I should think it would be more reasonable to have each one promise to try to be worthy of love and honor; that would at least be something one could work for.

Or how about having the bride promise to do all she can to achieve a serene and pleasant atmosphere in the home? That vow would be realistic and have a bit of sense to it, even if she never got very far toward accomplishing it. But there are many things she can do, with that goal in mind, if she cares to try.

It seems to me that a woman would be wise to try to find out in the first weeks of marriage, or even before, what her husband's idiosyncracies and special needs are. And she should tell him about hers. If a married couple are alike in certain things, such as stubbornness or lack of money sense, or if they both have been spoiled, they will run into a certain amount of difficulty. On the other hand, if they are quite different in various ways, there will be a lot of adjusting to do. The obvious things will soon be apparent: one likes to entertain and go to parties, the other doesn't; one may be neat, the other untidy, and so on. In these things and others that may appear, it shouldn't take so very long, with discussion and a willingness on both sides to be fair, to get on a good working basis.

But there are certain differences in the temperaments of married people that aren't so easily seen, are difficult to discuss, and can continue to be mildly upsetting through many years of a life together without either one realizing what the specific trouble is.

If the wife, say, is extravagant and there's a limited amount of money, this fault of hers will soon become apparent. Then there will be a showdown and no doubt some unpleasantness; she may have difficulty in reforming, but at least the thing is out in the open. However, let's say she has no feeling whatever for the most opportune time to make a remark, a request, a criticism or a suggestion. I know a woman who is both intelligent and considerate but who is sadly deficient in this sort of sensitiveness. Late at night when her husband is tired and anxious to get to bed and catch up on his sleep, she will ask him to do some little thing or other around the house, or will indulge in long-winded gossip or ask him for a considered opinion about something.

Unfortunately, her husband has an acute feeling that there's a proper and improper time for everything; not only is he careful not to criticize his wife when she's tired or upset, but also he knows enough to keep quiet when she's occupied with a job that requires some concentration. And being endowed with this sense of the appropriate, he's understandably annoyed by its absence in others, specifically in his wife.

There are many such differences in the temperaments of a couple which may be a continual source of irritation and annoyance. But it shouldn't be difficult and ought to be instructive to discuss each other's idiosyncracies. "Listen, dear, do you think you can remember not to talk to me when I'm trying to find out why the damned car won't go?" Or: "When I'm exhausted and trying to relax, please don't suggest that I call Aunt Sue at once," and so on.

Few people want to be irritating or to get on another's nerves, but it isn't easy to guess what annoys someone else, particularly if it's something that wouldn't disturb you in the least. So I believe it would help a lot if we were informed in advance.

Fred claims that he can tell what the general atmosphere around a home is just by observing the family's dog; he believes that tense, hectic people will make their dogs nervous and jumpy. Going along with this, it must follow that children, who are brought up by parents who don't get along, will definitely suffer from it. Many people, when they hear that a couple who has children are getting a divorce, feel that it's too bad because of the youngsters. Well, it is of course unfortunate for them to be deprived of a happy life with both parents, but if a woman can't live in reasonable contentment and peace with her husband, I certainly think she should leave him for the *sake* of the children, if for no other reason. It seems to me most unfair to bring tots into the world and then subject them to an unwholesome and disturbing atmosphere.

Wrangling and strife between wife and husband don't necessarily mean that there is a lack of love; on the contrary, affection may be the cause of quarrels if, for instance, jealousy is the main reason for the trouble. I know of no emotion more painful and none more difficult to master, whether or not there's any valid reason for it. Nor do I know of anyone who has been wise enough to say anything very helpful or constructive about jealousy, and I don't flatter myself that I can.

If you are a victim of this passion (in either of the two roles), it seems to me that there is little you can do except either make a complete break or put up with it, telling yourself that it can't last forever because nothing does. Growing older will help, for the most violent and painful forms of jealousy seem to be tied up with sex. This doesn't make sense to me, but as a species, human beings are immature and undeveloped, still fairly close to the mere animal. While we are advanced enough to have thought up a conception of love that is something more than merely sexual attraction, we can't seem to get away from the feeling that the two are closely connected. It's curious that this attitude should persist in a society in which so much sexual activity goes on with admittedly no love involved.

If a wife has a fleeting affair it is usually more disturbing to her husband (and vice versa) than if she is greatly drawn to some other man because she shares with him a profound enjoyment of music or literature or the theatre, or just because she finds great satisfaction in his companionship. Why is this? I imagine it is partly because so often young people get married only because they are sexually attracted to each other, mistaking this feeling for love.

Eventually, even though a husband and wife may still care for each other, their sex life may become nothing more than a quite uninspired habit. Then comes that dangerous age about which there are so many words spoken and written. The idea seems to be that married people get so used to each other that they become bored and begin to look around. My guess (and it is just that) is that it isn't only, nor even primarily, sex that they are looking for. With advancing years they are losing things they have felt were important: good looks, virility, youthfulness. Not having put anything else in their place the man (or woman) who is fast approaching middle age scrambles around desperately for something that will prove that he still has these precious assets.

Above all, a person wants to be understood. Many good and bad jokes have been made about the husband who strays because the other woman understands him. But no one understands anyone else, not even himself. It's a pathetically futile longing. And the woman at this age is also looking for romance. Being in love had been so thrilling, her heart beating faster at the sound of his voice, his step on the stair. Although many years of marriage can, and often do, give a couple something better and deeper than that other love, I doubt if there's any woman capable of getting excited and flushed when she hears a voice she has been listening to every day for twenty years.

What can we do about avoiding the pitfalls of the so-called dangerous age? I can't say anything about this from experience, because Fred and I were around that age when we married. We don't seem to have gotten around to being bored with each other, and at this stage of the game I guess our feeling is that we probably haven't got a lot of time left, so we had just better make the most of it. Of course, like any two people who marry at any age, we had to adjust to each other and it took us quite a while. Looking back, I can think of a few ways in which, by putting our minds to it and following a few simple rules, we could have reached our goal more quickly and painlessly.

A wise mother learns very soon to take into consideration the different temperaments of her children and to act accordingly. Why shouldn't a woman do the same with her husband? Of course there are times when we are depressed and almost anything would ruffle our feathers; according to our temperament, we will either snap at anyone who dares to speak to us or we will go around with a forbidding look, not voicing our bad feelings, but showing them nonetheless. A husband may either snap back, and perhaps a battle will get under way, or he may worry about what he has unwittingly done to offend. Fred and I take care of such a situation in this way: if either of us is out of sorts for no good reason, we announce it; the other one, learning that he isn't guilty, avoids all unnecessary conversation and is more considerate than usual until the clouds move on.

I have a theory that there's one constantly disturbing aspect for the woman who stays at home that is possibly harder on her than any other one thing, but which she may not be aware of. It is somewhat like an unceasing noise which gets on your nerves without your being actively conscious of it. I am referring to the fact that a housewife doesn't have definite and regular hours, such as evening, weekends, mealtimes, when she's completely separated from her job.

Anyone who has lived in the institution where he works knows there is something ingrown and suffocating about constantly seeing the same people day after day in the same environment. He has time off, it's true, just as most housewives do, but he does live, eat, and sleep with his job. There's no daily regularity nor certainty about any time completely away from his environment.

For the woman who stays at home, any conversation at breakfast may pertain to things a member of the family wants her to do: a suit should be sent to the cleaner's, that door should be fixed, and so on. Which means that now, even while she's eating, she's already on the job. Similarly at dinner and during the evening and through the weekend, there isn't likely to be much, if any, conversation about Father's work, unless it comes from his own desire to talk about it. But dozens of things relating to the wife's and mother's duties will pop up. Many women don't think about this aspect of their lives, and if it was brought to their attention they might say that they didn't mind it. But surely it is wearing, whether they realize it or not.

I remember once, shortly after we were married, Fred and I went to a quiet, pleasant restaurant for dinner and I was having a lovely time until Fred asked if I was going to send laundry out the next day. It was a shock. Maybe I'm unreasonable about this, but if you were at a party where one of your co-workers was also a guest and he asked you for a dance and in the midst of it wanted to know if you had remembered to type a letter, would you like it? Isn't it desirable for everyone to have definite times when he completely gets away from any thought of his job, however pleasant a one it may be? Isn't it only fair for the lady of the house to remind her family that business is business and is to be avoided when she's eating dinner or relaxing and reading in the evening?

I need insult no one's intelligence by discussing the obvious compromises which will surely have to be made in any marriage. And I suppose it's inevitable that the less selfish, more unspoiled one of the two will get the thin end of it. There are people who will announce that they have faults, but if you should try to pin them down to a specific shortcoming they can readily produce justification. If you're stuck with this sort of person for a husband, the only thing to do is to recognize it, accept it and relax. It's useless to try to make him see the light; you will just have to put up with it. If, for instance, you're the type who likes to be on time, and he's the sort who is always late, you can aggravate him and wear yourself out by trying to get him to start when you think you should. But it probably won't get you there any earlier, and you will both arrive in an unhappy frame of mind.

I know a woman who, through twenty-three years of marriage, has worked without ceasing at pushing her husband so she won't have to apologize, wherever they go, for being late. He simply will not co-operate, and when they arrive anywhere they both look upset. She could so much better have saved herself the unpleasantness, because their friends all know they will be late and the meal is arranged accordingly, or they are asked for a half hour earlier than anyone else. Everyone knows it isn't the woman's fault and the situation is accepted, but she continues to beat her head against a stone wall.

There are some people who won't discuss their faults with anyone; it is too unsavory a subject. Some of us can bear to have our failings brought to our attention, providing it isn't done in anger or in an obvious spirit of criticism. But many people have faults they aren't aware of, and a little constructive help in realizing them and getting rid of them may be appreciated by some offenders. Harping on anyone's shortcomings isn't going to get you very far, though. Even trying to tell someone how to get rid of a physical illness or pain is often futile and only produces antagonism. And since a person's faults are, to him, a more sensitive subject than a bodily ailment, it isn't surprising that he doesn't welcome discussions of them with eagerness.

The light touch is desirable, and an uncritical attitude is essential if you are going to get results. With youngsters whose faults needed curbing, I think I would be inclined to make a sort of game of it. Some general discussions might be in order, then some trading, such as, what do I do that you don't like? Well, I'll try to stop that if you will work on such and such that you do. Maybe, later, some voting and awards for those who had made real progress. The pitfall here could be that fault-finding and criticism might flourish, but I believe that danger could be avoided if the project wasn't undertaken too earnestly—but not too flippantly, either.

Even if I felt equipped to do so, I wouldn't expect to get very far in giving you any advice about handling your teen-agers, for it is you who have had them through their formative years. To do that job well, when you have fresh unspoiled material to work with, was relatively easy compared to what you may have on your hands now if you made a mess of their first years. If you didn't, you need no advice from anyone.

It seems to me that most people who give serious thought to the betterment of their relations with their family and friends approach it from one of two angles: either they set out to change the others somewhat, or they make an effort to accept large and small difficulties with better grace. I believe that the first method is a waste of time; trying to improve others, even assuming that you are wise enough to know what changes should be made, is a pretty dreary undertaking. The other system is all right as far as it goes, but I think a third should be added: a determination to stand for only so much lack of consideration and co-operation on the part of others.

Just as I think you can scarcely do anything worse to a child than to spoil it, so I believe you are doing nothing but harm to a person if you submit to a continued program of inconsiderate action from him. One thing in itself may be a trifle; perhaps your husband or son is inclined to drop a soiled shirt on the floor for you to pick up and put in the hamper. Or maybe someone always leaves a ring around the bathtub for you to clean.

Another woman might not mind these things, but I would, very much. In fact, I wouldn't stand for them. I would feel that I was being treated like a servant, and although I wouldn't mind taking a job as a maid (except that I would no doubt suffer the humiliation of being fired, since I'm not much good at housework), I could never get used to being treated like a servant by my husband and children. I wouldn't wrangle, however, because I hate above everything a quarreling household.

But the soiled clothes would be left there on the floor. I don't know how I would manage the problem of the dirty bathtub; perhaps I would settle for a sponge bath, or hire someone in to clean the tub, or leave home.

Of course I'm talking extravagantly, but the point I am trying to make is that if some member of your family is doing something that you know very well you will always resent every time it is done, you would both be better off if you put your foot down. I feel that you definitely do a disservice to a person if you ignore his acts of selfishness. So, even if you are pining to be a slave and a martyr, you shouldn't allow yourself that luxury.

Most of us have probably experienced the unfortunate circumstance of scarcely being able to stand the person who is married to someone we like immensely. But our own relatives, and particularly our husband's, may present an even worse problem, for they are less easy, if not impossible, to avoid. And since you do have to bear with them I think it's essential to face the thing at once and settle it in your mind, then act accordingly and treat it as a fact and not a problem.

I know a gentle and kindly young woman who suffered visitations from her own parents and those of her husband for the first few years of their marriage; I told her that she was actually a different person, and far from appealing, when these various relatives were around, and that for the sake of herself, husband, children and the parents themselves she should do something about a situation which made her seem so disagreeable. She got up her courage and told all of them to come to see her only when she invited them, and to remember, when visiting her, that it was *her* home, not theirs. Naturally there were some hurt feelings at first, but the strain for all of them soon disappeared, and for the past fifteen years they have actually enjoyed each other.

Our relations with our friends are easier to establish and handle, and yet what a lot of time and money one can spend going through motions that bring no real satisfaction to anyone! Take the business of a bread-and-butter letter, for instance. Such letters carry no conviction, since one is supposed to write and say one had a lovely visit, whether it's true or not. Why waste time on such a meaningless gesture? To almost everyone I know, sending Christmas cards is a headache and an expense in both money and time, just when most people are short of both of those commodities; the cards also have little significance, since most senders simply get out a list of names which they hurriedly copy on envelopes, wishing all the while that they could skip the job.

I don't care for sweets, so I usually don't want dessert and even if it's something I like I've probably had enough already. There are two things that give me indigestion: one is overeating and the other is eating something I don't much like. Most of this is no doubt psychological, but the pain is the same, whether it's from the food or from my attitude to it. So I often turn down my hostess's final offering. I would rather *she* would be upset than I, since she will recover sooner. And by now most of them take my refusal for granted.

This works all the way up and down the line. You can quietly but firmly make your own rules and most people will just accept them and probably think none the less of you for them. Once I said to a new acquaintance that I honestly didn't care what anyone thought about what I did or didn't do, and he replied, "Then there's something wrong somewhere, because any normal person wants others to like him and, if possible, admire him. Why, I want our elevator boy, whose name I don't even know, to think I'm a nice guy."

But he had misunderstood me, I am just as pleased as anyone else when people like me, but I definitely don't care whether or not they approve of my behavior. If they dislike me because I think it's a waste of time to write a bread-and-butter letter, they are welcome to do so. In other words, I prefer to be liked for what I am, rather than for a role I play, particularly if it's one I didn't think up myself.

Taking a stand, saying No when that is what you want to say, is something like a surgical operation—not pleasant to look forward to, no fun to undergo, but in many cases exactly the thing that will get desirable results. Trying to accept a situation you dislike is a strain and is hard on you and everyone around you. It may take a little courage to have a tooth pulled, or to radically change some aspect of your life that you definitely dislike, but everyone concerned will probably benefit if you can summon that courage. At least *you* will be better off, and if you have the worthy ambition to be kind and considerate to everybody, why exclude yourself?

XI

The Hand That Rules the Cradle Rocks the World

I DON'T have any children of my own, but I happened to be the middle one among nine of us in our family. So, in a way, I have had some, and my brother Donald, twelve years my junior, was my special charge. Since then I've been very close to my sister's three children—Juanita, Roger, and Virginia—and, like so many innocent bystanders, I've had plenty of opportunity to observe mothers and their offspring in action. Anyhow, while I may not be the most qualified person in the world to offer comments and suggestions in this sphere, I'm going to go ahead and do it, because I believe that many women fail to apply simple common sense to the problems that arise.

Recently I was present when three young mothers, each hoping to have several children, were discussing whether or not it was better to have them quite close together or to space them, say three or four years apart, and one said, "I would rather have them far apart, for then you can really enjoy each one," and I blurted out, "Oh, my word, I didn't know you were expecting to *enjoy* them!"

They all laughed, but I was serious; if the mothers I know enjoy their babies they manage to do it when I'm not around. Moreover, one would never guess from their outspoken attitude toward the business of coping with their youngsters that there was much pleasure in it.

Bringing up children is a demanding job and little short of unceasing. Even when you leave a trustworthy sitter at home, you are still in charge. If your host's telephone rings, you become alert; is the call for you? Did the baby swallow a toy, or is he running a high temperature, or is the house on fire? But if you mothers agree with me that bringing up children is also the most important job there is, then I should think that you would be resigned to the fact that the hours are longer and the strain and anxieties greater than if you had chosen to work at a desk or behind a counter. Yet many of you seem to spend time and energy resenting, or at least deploring, the whole state of affairs.

A humble filing clerk has to stick right at it from nine to five; why should a mother expect more freedom than an office worker? The obvious reply to this is that she doesn't get anything like as much freedom, for she doesn't have evenings and weekends to do with as she pleases. Well, true to some extent, except that with normal, healthy, well-trained children she should be able to enjoy those evenings she spends at home and, with the help of a baby sitter or a co-operative husband, get away from it all now and then. She may even snatch an hour here and there through the day, which is something an office worker can't do. If you compare any two jobs or situations, one will always have advantages and disadvantages that the other hasn't.

When we arrive at a certain time in our lives the majority of us are faced with the necessity of working if we want to stay alive; we have no choice. However, we do have a choice when it comes to having children. Once having had a baby, we may be sorry, but it's too late to change our minds. And even in their most harassed moments most mothers would choose to keep their children. Therefore it seems to me that they should pay the price with some show of cheerfulness. There are so many situations in which the sufferer had no voice in the matter.

Actually, I have never been able to pin any mother down to telling me exactly what she is so busy at all day. What about all those modern conveniences? Washing machines, a real time-saver, some women simply shrug off, claiming that they spend as much time washing as their grandmothers did because they wash clothes several times a week and sometimes every day.

But these modern housewives know little or nothing about old-time washday. They don't realize that Grandma had to carry in water from the well and heat it on a wood or coal fire which had to be kept going. She had to rub each piece on a washboard, then empty the soapy water out of doors and carry in more water for rinsing. It's true that when I describe all this to some young mothers they do seem to be sorrier for Grandma than they are for themselves, and that is just about as sorry as anyone can get. Still, they have no conception of such things as filling lamps with kerosene, trimming the wicks, washing the lamp chimneys, tending a fire in the cooking stove, heating water for baths. Apropos of modern conveniences in general, one young mother recently said to me, "The telephone and the car take up so much of our time that they cancel the good of all the others."

Once when I was trying to find out from one of these young women what she had to do as compared to what Grandma did, I told her of someone I knew who brought up four children some fifty years ago in the pre-gadget era. There was little money and this mother did all the housework and laundry. She also made her own dresses and all of the children's clothes. She made her husband's shirts, did endless mending, yet often had time to toss off a dress for one of her sisters. The meals were good, the house was clean and tidy, and by three o'clock every afternoon she and the children had all taken naps, were washed and dressed, and were playing or reading while they waited for Father to come home.

She was a good organizer, but more important, I think, was the fact that the children minded her the first time she spoke, not the twenty-first. Not only did they pick up their own toys and clothes, but they also picked up after the baby. Beginning when they were hardly more than babies themselves, their mother gave them the feeling that their help was important to her, although no doubt at first she spent a good deal of her valuable time letting them "help." It paid off. One evening when the parents had gone out to dinner, leaving the children with an aunt, the three-year-old daughter said, "Which shall we do first, Aunt Emma? Wash the dishes or put the boys to bed?"

At this point in the story my friend exclaimed explosively, "I *hate* that woman!"

I don't know what her little outburst means to you; to me it meant that that young mother, and apparently many others, are caught in some kind of a whirlpool and don't know what to do about it.

Children's and mothers' temperaments differ; certainly all children can't be handled alike to advantage. But I do profoundly believe that there is one rule which applies to any normal child and probably to many who aren't quite normal. I think it's tremendously important for a child to know where he stands and a mother who says No and Don't twenty times a day but carries it through only five times is making life more difficult for herself and, I should think, more confusing for the child. If one time you call an apple an apple and the next time an orange, what is a child supposed to think it is?

My main suggestion to a young mother is: be stingy with your prohibitions; never say No or Don't unless it's so important that you are sure you will stand pat. If your child wants to play with a dangerously sharp knife or a box of matches, the answer is No, and my guess is that you'll follow it through and see to it that he doesn't cut his little brother's throat or burn the house down. If you have enough character to make him obey when it's vitally important, what's wrong about being *consistent* about making him mind?

Some friends of ours dropped in to see us one Sunday afternoon, bringing their four-year-old boy with them. Fred had a new record which they wanted to hear, but before he played it, he put on some birdcalls for the child, then, when the other record had been played, the boy asked to hear the birdcalls again. His father said No, they wanted to talk now, and he tried to get the child to play with the toys they had brought along.

The boy kept on pestering Fred and his father; finally I called him over to me and said, "You want to hear the birds again, don't you?" Eagerly he nodded and I went on, "But when you asked them, Fred and your father said No. Do you know what that means? It means they aren't going to play the record again because they want to talk and it's too noisy. So why don't you just play with that cute rabbit you brought?"

"Oh, they'll play the record," he answered with complete confidence. "If I keep on asking and asking they'll get tired and play it."

The father and mother looked at each other in consternation; this was their fourth child, and they hadn't learned yet that youngsters are onto their parents and know how to handle them.

Now if a child is as quick as that to learn how to get what he wants, we can assume that it's relatively easy to teach him that he *can't* get it by teasing, disobeying and wearing us down. Two mothers I know can take their little ones into anybody's home without having to spend all their time on the edge of their chairs, ready to jump up and rescue something from the child. They started when the tots were first able to crawl to a table and begin to grab and taught them that they mustn't touch anything without permission. These mothers admitted that this took a few full days of constant surveillance, but it seemed to them a small price to pay for peace at home and abroad. Moreover, the child is happier. There is enough time ahead in which he will have to face frustration, disappointment and the displeasure of others, without submitting to those things prematurely.

I wish that the mothers who love their offspring in an unthinking and over-sentimental way, determinedly giving them everything they want and letting them do almost everything they want to do, would realize that almost certainly they aren't doing the child a favor. Teaching him not to handle everything in sight, showing him how to dress himself, insisting that he put his toys away and, a little later but not much later, giving him jobs to do which will make him feel that he is a help and not a nuisance—these things take time and patience. However, compared to the time and patience which will otherwise be a drain on you through several years to come, they take very little. If you start early enough, I think you will be surprised at how soon your child will learn to be neat, obedient and helpful.

Teaching and nagging are two different things, however, and the latter is surely an unpleasantness to be avoided in any household. In our big family of nine children it may have been the Quaker influence which kept the atmosphere relatively peaceful. Not only are Quakers against organized warfare, but also they don't go for impromptu hit-and-miss battles inside the family circle, particularly between stronger and weaker powers such as adults and children.

We youngsters had a normal amount of warfare among ourselves, as I remember, but we were rarely scolded and were punished almost not at all. I never saw Mother in a temper and didn't see her cry more than two or three times in my life. In her treatment of her children she followed insofar as possible the Quaker doctrine of letting us be guided by our own Inner Light. But I never heard her say that she did this; she didn't practice what she preached—she practiced without preaching. When we were doing wrong she didn't tell us to stop; she would just put us to work at something, or send us on an errand, which automatically stopped us. This wasn't punishment to us, and I was grown up before I figured out that it was all just a neat trick.

If the children have a playroom of their own it might be a good idea to let them be masters of it. Just as you insist on having things your way in your part of the house, perhaps they might be allowed to have their way in their own domain. If there are several children there will be arguments and squabbles but, unless some older, stronger child is a tyrant, insofar as possible I would let them thrash things out without my interference. In their own room, however; no battles in my territory.

One trouble with reading books of advice on this important subject is that the "authorities" don't agree. We were visiting our niece, Virginia, several years ago when her youngest was about two months old. After dinner we were all in the living room when we heard the baby crying. Virginia started to get up, sat down, then got up again, saying, "Well, excuse me a minute. The last book I read you pick them up when they cry."

In one book I've seen, a doctor says that people should wait until they are thirty-five years old to have children, because, before that age, they aren't mature enough to do the job properly in all its aspects. But in my observation many people aren't mature when they're seventy, let alone when they're thirty-five. Common sense is perhaps the most important asset in a parent, and a twenty-year-old may well have more of that commodity than his grandparents.

For another thing, surely we will agree that the older we get the harder it is on us, nervously, to be around children, particularly in these days when discipline has fallen by the wayside. If you begin to have children at the age of thirty-five and have four of them, two years apart, you will be fifty by the time the youngest has reached the age of seven. Can you cope? All I have to do to believe that you can't do this happily is to look around at the grandparents I know.

My sister Juanita had four children and now has nine grandchildren. And now, to make my point, I had better admit that she was the woman I told about at the beginning of this chapter, the one who taught her children to obey and be a help. I didn't say who it was, because I didn't want to seem to be boasting about my own family, but now, in telling about her relations with her grandchildren, it's significant to know that she was an unusually capable mother. Also a casual one in the best sense, I think.

But with her grandchildren my sister is far from casual, worrying over them as she never did over her own children. Not long ago she telephoned me from Long Island to ask me to be sure to see that Roger and his wife, who were going to spend the weekend with us, started home early on Sunday, since they were leaving their children at home with the oldest, seventeen, in charge. It was unlike her to call me for such a thing and I said so, and she laughed and replied, "Oh, don't pay the slightest attention to me; I know I'm ridiculous. Every night when you go to bed thank God that you aren't a grandmother. Grandmothers have no sense."

Yet, with all this devotion she, as well as many other grandparents whom I've observed and even questioned on the subject, can stand her grandchildren only in small doses. One at a time, by preference, and then not for a very long stretch. The fact is that the older we get the less we enjoy being around small children, even if they are well-behaved. A normal child is noisy and almost constantly in motion, which is wearing for a person who has lived long enough to need, and to know the value of, quiet and relaxation. As for young mothers—well, I recently read about a doctor who said that in general what is wrong with mothers is that they're "pooped." Don't give them a tranquilizer, he advised; give that to the children and the husband.

Everybody is sorry for a child whose parents are separated or divorced, and I am, too, for the usual reasons, and for yet another one: I have seen divorced parents (and some who aren't) trying so hard to keep the major share of the child's love that they will go to detrimental lengths in spoiling it. Each parent wants to be first in its affection, and will give in to its every demand in spite of the fact that a child doesn't necessarily love best the person it can exploit most easily.

Even if we get a good break, it's a wonder to me how any of us grow up without being self-centered. I once happened to see on a New York sidewalk a little girl surrounded by five or six adults who were admiring her new shoes, of which she was obviously very proud. All that rapt interest in us, then we grow up and who cares whether we have new shoes or not? That was my thought then, and just this moment another one came to me: could this sort of attention when we are very young be in part responsible for our undue concern, all through our lives, with what others think about what we wear, or do, or possess? Page the psychologists!

Just one more gratuitous comment: I think many parents worry too much about their children's faults, by which I don't mean their behavior; in that, I fear, they do a bit of neglecting. I mean that in almost any child we can, I believe, find indications of dishonesty, deceit, and most of the other sins of mankind. We all have seeds of good and evil in us, and as the years go by most of us fall into some kind of middle path; saints and hardened criminals are the exception. Therefore, if your child seems normal and has two decent parents, I think you may safely ignore the tendency he may show now and then toward landing in jail.

I will use my niece, Virginia, as an example. She was just under three years old when, one day, her brother Roger came into the room where she and I were and began to tease her. My back was to them. Suddenly I heard a crash, turned around, and saw her glass of milk lying broken at Roger's feet. Answering the look of surprise and I don't know what other expression on my face, she smiled with almost unbelievable sweetness and innocence and, glancing at her brother, said, "Did you fro' that glass, Roger?"

The makings of a little criminal, surely; lying, deceitful, putting the blame for her act on someone else! Some mothers, faced with this incident and others like it, might be afraid they had a future gun moll on their hands. I hardly need add that Virginia grew up to be a normal, decent citizen; if she hadn't, I wouldn't have told that story.

I think that bringing up children is by far the most exacting job in the world. If you are running a country, for instance, you can take weekends off sometimes, perhaps go on a vacation; you're not likely to be called to duty in the middle of the night, and you seldom have to get up earlier in the morning than you intended. To do a good job is difficult, but you have experts to consult and many people to help and advise you.

Well, if you're a mother you, too, can consult experts and get advice, but the trouble, as I've mentioned, is that the experts are constantly changing their minds and contradicting each other. So in the end you must rely largely on yourself. Don't forget that you got the children into this predicament, but if you do the best you can, as cheerfully as you can, the chances are they may never reproach you for bringing them into the world.

My final word is this: don't expect your child to be better than you are. If you never under any circumstances tell the smallest lie, are never unreasonable, never out of sorts, never raise your voice, are always gentle, polite, considerate and have beautiful manners, perhaps your example is enough.

XII

Does Your Garden Grow?

The majority of people who love to garden get a thrill out of it and are, in one respect, somewhat like those who truly love music or paintings or fine literature. That is, they are uplifted, and even sometimes feel that this exaltation puts them a cut above others who have no special liking for their particular enthusiasm. There is, however, this difference: a person may feel superior if he merely enjoys concerts, or art museums, or Shakespeare, while a gardener must do the work himself (at least some of it) in order to get the full benefit of that somewhat holier-than-thou feeling.

Fortunately, anyone who wants to can, to some extent or other, grow something. Even if the only space you have is a sunny windowsill, you can, for a small sum, have a geranium or begonia which will probably bloom for you. If you have no sunny window, get a gardenia plant or something else that will thrive in the shade.

If you have no money at all to spare for a plant you could, first, help yourself to some dirt in the park; I don't believe you would be arrested for swiping a small amount of dirt, but if you're afraid you might be, try to find a policeman who looks human and ask him if you may have it. Then, if you can't afford to buy a flowerpot, punch a small hole in the bottom of a tin can and put the dirt in it.

Now, since you're alive, we can assume that you eat, so buy yourself some food that has a seed in it and put the seed into the soil. If nothing happens, try another kind. The day will come when something will sprout for you, and if you care enough to go through all this, I would be willing to bet that the seed that sprouts and lives, even for a little while, because of you, will give you a bigger thrill than a vast assortment of expensive and beautiful plants grown by somebody else.

After I had gardened here in Poverty Hollow for fourteen years by the old-fashioned hard-work method, I suddenly thought up a system which is in some ways more successful and which does away with most of the labor. As a result of my method, my flower and vegetable gardens haven't had to be plowed or spaded for sixteen years. There are practically never any weeds to cope with. I don't hoe or cultivate or wear myself out making a compost pile.

The simple answer is that my plot is constantly covered with hay, leaves, sawdust, wood chips, garbage (all but meat scraps which attract animals)—in short, with any vegetable matter that rots. This not only outwits weeds and holds the moisture in the soil, but also keeps the ground soft. And, by constantly rotting, the mulch enriches the soil to such a degree that the only fertilizer of any kind that I have used for the past fourteen years is cottonseed meal or soybean meal to supply nitrogen.

My system is a form of organic gardening, but that isn't the point I make in the book I wrote about it, or in articles, or in talks to garden clubs and other groups. Actually, I started my method before I'd ever heard of organic gardeners, and not until long after I'd been practicing their theory did I realize that I was one of them.

In any event, there's a distinct difference between my kind of organic gardening and the original orthodox variety. The old-timers still plow and cultivate, and it seems to me that they work harder than many of the really old-fashioned farmers, although I have no doubt that they get better results. But I'm afraid they pay a high price in time and strength and money. The compost pile, for instance, seems to be an absolute necessity in their program, and that alone is a big job. Also, they feed their soil with all kinds of organic fertilizers, which takes both time and money.

What I really want to point out here, though, is that by the method I use, a busy mother, a woman who works all day at a job or one who spends only weekends in the country can grow both flowers and vegetables with so little labor that she need never feel driven. And unless you have to grow food from dire necessity, it seems a bit incongruous to do it if it makes you tense, nervous or over-tired. As for flowers, if there's one thing in the world that should bring us serenity rather than strain, it's a fragrant blossom.

Now if you want to go further and enjoy your own vegetables all winter from your freezer, it's unbelievably little added work. When I first read the instructions which tell you that everything you freeze must be perfect, I thought well, naturally; who would go to the trouble to freeze a product that was too young or too old or inferior in some other way? I did do it a time or two, though, and found out for myself how foolish it is.

There are one or two ways, however, in which I think I've improved on the rules. They say, for example, that beets don't freeze satisfactorily, and they don't if you do them the way they tell you to. But I cook a big pot of them until tender, skin them, cool, slice and freeze. Or don't slice. Or make them into Harvard beets and freeze. Or pickle them and freeze. These are all just like freshly-cooked beets when you serve them weeks or months later. And if your family happens to prefer some vegetables served cold, as salad, you can cook those vegetables just until tender, cool and freeze; when you want to serve them, take them out in time to thaw, use whatever salad dressing you like, and that's all there is to it. By the way, try putting a really generous dab of French or German mustard into the dressing for a variation.

A few nutritionists and experts on freezing have jumped on me for such procedures, because apparently you lose vitamins and flavor doing vegetables this way. Well, each of us can make up his own mind whether or not we lose enough flavor to matter. As for vitamins, the women who feed their children all sorts of food that has no value are hardly going to care, and the conscientious ones can perhaps afford to skip a vitamin once in a while.

If you pick corn at exactly the right time (not too young, not too old) and get it into the freezer in a matter of a few minutes, you will find that you lose no flavor. It won't be as crisp as fresh corn, however. Last summer somebody told me that if you pick it and don't husk it (don't even peek to see if there's a worm around), wrap it and put it in the freezer, you will really have something. I didn't get to try it, but I am planning to go to the corn patch next summer with some freezer paper, wrap a few ears on the stalk, pull them off and run like mad to the freezer. It will be interesting to see what the outcome is, my guess being that the flavor will be wonderful but the crispness missing. That is, I *was* planning to do that, but just now Professor Richard Clemence, whom I am inclined to believe no matter what he says, tells me that corn holds its flavor better if it's husked the minute it's picked. So take your choice.

I have been told that you can freeze parsley simply by putting fresh sprigs of it into polyethylene plastic bags and putting them into the freezer. When it's growing in the garden my sister Mary and I eat great bouquets of it, yet I've been tempted only once to try freezing it. But I ground it up first, thinking that the other way would take up too much room. A neighbor happened to drop in while I was grinding and came back the next day with a whole bushel of parsley. Being incapable of throwing out anything so fresh and desirable and reeking with vitamins, I ground up every bit of it. And this may sound incredible, but when he returned a few days later with another half-bushel, I ground that too and put it into the freezer.

The outcome of all this was that I took to seasoning everything lavishly with parsley; I knew I was overdoing it, but there it was, so much of it, and I couldn't restrain myself. However, when Fred began saying "Please pass the parsley" at mealtimes I had to reform, because I didn't know which dish to pass. (A friend has suggested that I call this book *Poor Fred,* and I have to admit that it would be appropriate.)

Of course I freeze our own Fairfax strawberries. And raspberries. And blueberries if I'm in the mood to pick some wild ones. You can freeze applesauce satisfactorily but I seldom do it, since we can buy Cortland apples all winter long, a half bushel at a time.

You can keep rhubarb all winter by cutting it up and putting it, raw, into Mason jars. Cover it with cold water, seal, and store in the cellar. If your family doesn't care for rhubarb, and you have the notion that it's good for them, they will probably like it this way:

RHUBARB JUICE

Fill a good-sized pot nearly to the top with rhubarb cut into two-inch lengths and cover with cold water. Add a little nutmeg or vanilla, if you wish. Or both. Bring to a boil and simmer until fruit is soft. Remove from fire. Sweeten to your taste, preferably with honey.

If you let it cool a little it is somewhat easier to handle. Put a piece of cheesecloth into a large strainer or sieve, strain the fruit, and you have a beautifully colored juice. Many people don't know what it is when they taste it, and I have never found anyone, even those who dislike rhubarb, who doesn't like this juice. If you grow your own rhubarb and have freezer space, you can have a delicious drink all year round. Or just can it.

Have you ever eaten milkweed? It will pinch-hit for both lettuce and asparagus. Locate a spot where it grows, and when it gets from eight to twelve inches high pull it up, pinch off the top two or four little leaves to add to a green salad, cut off the tough bottom end, and cook the rest of the stem as you would asparagus. If there's enough around you can freeze it for winter use.

We eat asparagus almost daily during the season; it's one vegetable we don't tire of. You have to pick it (don't cut it—snap it off) every day or it will get too old, and I usually get enough each time for two or three meals. I freeze what we don't eat that day. It probably takes about five minutes to freeze two meals of it. Is someone protesting that this can't be true, since the steaming alone takes five minutes? Yes, it does, but I don't have to stand and watch it steam; perhaps I set the table for dinner. Are you going to count that against the time that I myself have to forfeit?

The same holds true with a large head of cauliflower (white or purple) or more broccoli picked than we need for that night's dinner. To cook enough carrots, beets, kohlrabi so that I will have two or three extra meals to put in the freezer will take only an additional few minutes. Last fall I prepared a huge head of sweet and sour cabbage which took perhaps twenty minutes longer than if I had made enough for only one meal, but it filled ten containers, ready to serve except for thawing and heating. Two minutes to a meal.

From all I've been saying about saving time in gardening, cooking, freezing and cleaning house, one might get the idea that I hate to work. I don't. Much as I enjoy reading and seeing my friends, the hours when I'm working are the ones I like best, possibly because I get infinite satisfaction out of accomplishment. But of course I have preferences. I would rather scrub the kitchen floor than use the vacuum in the living room, rather plant the garden than pick the crop. I suppose the truth is that I enjoy changing something for the better. The fun in washing a window, for instance, lies in the obvious improvement, and I'm afraid that I let mine wait until there's no doubt about the need for improvement.

More seriously, though, I love to make something appear where nothing was, such as a brilliant bed of verbenas or a poem. Even a second-rate poem; I don't know what it feels like to produce a fine one. But I have produced a beautiful head of cabbage, an almost startling bed of *phlox drummondi,* and peonies. I think if I had to name my favorite flower it would be a white single peony; as long as I have a few of these each June, I feel that I need go no further than our own yard to enjoy as much beauty and fragrance as anyone has a right to in a long lifetime.

And now, once again, the theme song: your garden, like everything else in your life, should be aimed at suiting you and your family. If nobody else ever saw your lawn, would you be upset because it wasn't up to the highest standard? If you wouldn't, then relax, call it a yard instead of a lawn, eat what dandelions you can, admire them while they're in flower, and when they go to seed, look in some other direction.

XIII

To Hell with the Joneses

If you were to sit down and take stock of all your actions, you might come to the conclusion that you always do as you want to, *under the circumstances.* But if you wish things were different, the answer is to change the circumstances, and this will probably mean, above all, changing your attitude. Circumstances aren't only physical; they are also what goes on in your mind.

From my own experience I can practically promise you that you won't lose anyone's affection or respect if you decide to belong to yourself instead of allowing yourself to be torn up and handed around in little pieces, each so small that it isn't of much use to anybody. Again it comes back to the same old thing: why on earth don't we do our own thinking and follow through with actions?

When I was in high school our English teacher asked us which play of Shakespeare's we liked best. For some reason I was just then enamored of *Julius Caesar* and chose that one, hardly noticing that everyone else was picking *Hamlet* or some slightly lesser piece. The teacher looked at me approvingly and said, "Good! I like to find a pupil with an unorthodox opinion, and brave enough to express it."

I was inordinately pleased with that praise, though I didn't deserve it, since bravery hadn't entered in. All through the years I have followed my own inclinations—Mother's belief in letting people follow their Inner Light really took with me. For instance, I had my hair bobbed immediately after Irene Castle put the idea into my head, and long before anyone else cut theirs. You young women probably can't imagine how I was stared at and how it upset people. However, nobody stopped speaking to me, and eventually most females visited the barber and then it was all right; everybody was doing it.

Could there be anything more unsatisfying or futile than to try to live our lives, either in little or big things, according to the standards of others? Must I wear a hat because other people do? Is that reason enough? Must I be loyal to someone or something because public opinion says I should? Then what happens when two loyalties conflict? It seems to me there can be only one sensible reason for wearing a hat: because you want to. And surely there can be only one loyalty: to the best you feel and know within yourself.

Let's consider the matter of styles, for example. If you try to keep up with the Joneses long enough it may well become a habit, and perhaps the time will come when you can no longer distinguish clearly between the things you do because you want to and those you do because others are doing them. When a style as noticeable as the sack dress comes along it attracts so many jibes that you might defy it. But other styles which you may not like much come and go, and they may be unbecoming to you, yet you buy and wear them, scarcely realizing that you do it because you'll look out of style if you don't. Recently I heard that wigs were the fashion, and just think how a girl would suffer if she were *obliged* to wear a wig!

You may think that you wear high heels because you consider them attractive, but let them no longer be the thing and my guess is that you'd abandon them. Most "dress" shoes can affect your very expression, so if you see a woman with an anguished look on her face, don't jump to the conclusion that her heart is breaking until you glance at her feet; it may be only the shoes she's wearing. Nor is she necessarily drunk because she wobbles around a good deal when she walks.

A woman who didn't know me very well once said to me, "I imagine that if you were invited to a party so formal that you couldn't wear sandals or low heels you wouldn't go."

While I was puzzling over that deep problem, Fred answered for me, "Oh, she'd go all right if she wanted to, but she'd wear low heels and wouldn't know she wasn't supposed to. Or even if she did know, you couldn't possibly convince her that anyone would notice what kind of shoes she had on, or that if they did they would give a damn."

Recently some young women I was talking to got on to the subject of dress, and they actually seemed to think that women no longer paid much attention to the styles. I can't prove that they were mistaken, but wouldn't styles stop changing so often and drastically if women didn't co-operate? I have been told by women who say they would prefer not to conform that you are more or less helpless if you need a new outfit and can't sew. However unbecoming the current style may be to you, that's what is being sold and therefore that's what you buy.

Some years ago I went to a large, fashionable camp in the Adirondacks; an old friend of mine owned it and she had asked me to go up for the month of September to straighten out her bookkeeping system. One of her employees met me at the train; I was carrying one very small suitcase, and he asked about my trunk. I said I didn't bring one.

"But—your luggage?" he asked.

"Here it is," and I handed him the little bag.

During the month he and I became friendly, and toward the end of it he said to me, "I never felt sorrier for anyone in my life than I did for you the day I met you at the train. You were going to be at a place for a whole month where the girls try to wear a different dress every day and doll up for the evenings, and you had only one little bag. I know now what you had in it: two sweaters and two pairs of bloomers. And you wander around in those clothes, not giving a damn, and now I never envied anyone so much."

He went on, perhaps too scornfully, about the girls who had brought so many clothes. It's conceivable that they enjoyed dressing up, so why not? However, he was an observant and intelligent man and the point is that he was sure any girl would inevitably suffer in that environment if she couldn't conform. I like to wear pretty clothes, but sweaters and bloomers had seemed the easiest and most practical solution on that occasion.

The last night I was there the guests had a sort of farewell party. We were gathered around a big bonfire. I was wearing the dress I had traveled in, and I made a little speech, all about how wonderful our hostess was, how much I owed her, how I would do anything in the world for her, make any sacrifice. It was so flowery and so overdone that it was a little embarrassing to my friend and to the audience until I came to the end and the big gesture: knowing, I said, how she had suffered the whole month over my appearance, I was going to destroy the offending articles, and I tossed the bloomers onto the fire. It was about time for them to retire, anyway.

I never liked slacks but I used to wear them in very cold weather. When we first moved to the country Fred flattered me by buying me a pair of skis when he got some for himself. I think I put them on only once and spent most of the time flat on my face. He also bought me a ski suit, and during those first cold winters I was in it most of my waking hours. One of our neighbors told me once that I wore more clothes in winter and fewer in summer than anyone she'd ever known.

One cold snowy day Fred and I went to New York, and among other things I had a dentist's appointment. I wore the ski suit and it almost wrecked me; the dentist was doing something important in my mouth when he suddenly noticed the pants, gave a yelp of surprise and dropped his tool. This will give you some idea of how long ago it was; I guess that pants on a woman, even in a dentist's chair, would cause little excitement today. Again, it's all right because others do it.

I also went here and there in shorts long before anyone else did. Fred claims that not only did I go shopping in Danbury in them but that I also often wore a pajama top with them. He may be right, but it sounds a little unlikely to me unless the pajamas were unusually attractive; after all, I have my share of vanity.

Because of all the remarks that were made about my mode of dressing, I became, if not self-conscious, at least conscious. So one day when I was going to call on a neighbor whom I had met only a couple of times and who was, I guess, a lady in both the best and worst senses of that word, I did stop to think about what to wear and, deliberately, chose shorts. I could have happily put on a clean dress instead but I figured somewhat like this: I will probably live in this neighborhood the rest of my life, and I may or may not build up good relationships with the people who live near us. But in any case I am not going to let them be any kind of burden on me—that is, clutter up my life with superficial values.

I had thought about this for quite a while, but I told Fred my conclusion in one sentence when he saw me starting out to call on this neighbor. I said, "I've decided to do what I feel like doing and not what's expected of me. For the rest of my life, I mean."

He laughed and replied, "Well, you've got along all right that way so far. Anyway, you would never be able to figure out what was expected of you. And if anyone told you, you wouldn't believe it."

Probably he was right and, for the most part, no one bothers to tell me, although during the past twenty years there's been quite a to-do over my favorite pocketbook. It is made of soft pliable black leather and has a clasp of dull-colored brass, and in its youth no doubt it was able to hold up its head in any gathering. Even when I got it (I don't remember whose hand-me-down it was), it wasn't noticeably objectionable by anyone's standard, but that was quite a few years ago. I didn't notice, but

I suppose it did begin to show wear and tear as time went on. Don't we all? On my birthday about ten years ago Fred gave me an expensive and, I think, handsome handbag, but it was too big and too stiff for my taste and I asked him to exchange it for a suitcase which I did need.

A year or so later a friend saw me taking money out of my comfortable old handbag for the fruit and vegetable man who comes to the house, and she gave me a slightly used one of her own to take its place. Now my system is to accept gifts graciously whether I want them or not; I can always find someone to give them to. I presented this one to a neighbor who seemed to appreciate it. My own old bag suited me and I clung to it. Later, someone else gave me a new bag; I gave it away. In a year or so another friend presented me with a huge and gorgeous affair, which one of my sisters liked a lot; she got it. Others have trickled in since; I won't try to list them. They all found happy owners.

I will admit that now, even by my standards, the old reliable looks as though it had been through quite a lot, but it still serves, and even in its heyday I didn't carry it when I was what I call dressed up. Now the old bag accompanies me only when I go marketing, and if the butcher and grocer disapprove of it, they are too well-mannered to let on.

My guess is that this pocketbook and I will give up the ghost simultaneously, but I don't ask that it be buried with me; my attachment to it isn't a sentimental one. The other side of the coin is that I am also past master in the art of elimination. I did away with tablecloths by the same process of reasoning I used against hats: they were unnecessary. But for the past ten years or so, on Thanksgiving Day, we use an old, worn, red and white cloth, the kind your great-grandmother used, and once one of our guests said, "You never did tell us the history of this lovely old cloth; it must have one."

"It has, rather," I answered. "One day I told our laundryman that I'd heard that laundries often had old rags around, which they had no use for, and if he had any surplus ones I'd be obliged if he'd give them to me. Besides this tablecloth, there were a few other choice items in what he brought me."

I like the cloth for itself and because it reminds me of my childhood, but not enough to wash and iron it myself; I send it to the laundry, and if some day they get mixed up and give it to somebody else for an old rag—well, I shall have had my turn.

Television is in another category, for it serves a definite purpose; it must be a great boon to sick or lonely people who enjoy it, and for this let's give it a high mark. We haven't a set, so I'm going to express no opinion of it but merely report a few facts and observations. When we meet someone else who hasn't one, he treats us as if he and we were something special. Why? And here's a more interesting question: why do many who do have a set, hearing that we haven't one, begin to apologize for theirs, and seem to be almost ashamed of it? Or why do they try to make a case for it?

Now and then someone with a set has told us how much we are missing, and has insisted on trying to prove it. Some neighbors, for instance, invited us to their home especially to listen to a program they highly recommended. As we started out Fred said to me, "Want to bet that as soon as it's over they'll say it wasn't as good as usual?"

We arrived, saw the program, and at the end of it both husband and wife exclaimed, "It wasn't so good tonight. Usually it's *much* better than that."

And this seems to be our fate; when *we* watch, a program falls down on the job.

Here's another aspect of the T.V. situation: parents in general seem to think that their children watch it more than is good for them, and one of their reasons seems to be that it's a passive thing rather than an active one. Mothers often admit shamefacedly that they permit this static situation because it keeps the children out from underfoot. And parents say they can't refuse to have a set because their children's friends all have them. One mother had their set put in the attic, where the children can't stand the cold in winter or the heat in summer. I personally have nothing against T.V., just as, personally, I have nothing against earthquakes. So far I haven't been inconvenienced by either one.

To go on to other fields, I wish some psychiatrist would explain to me what goes on in the minds of people who hire someone to decorate their houses or landscape their gardens. To me that department in life seems so simple: either you have taste of some kind and know what you like and want to live with, or you haven't and therefore you don't care what your surroundings are like.

Do you fix up your house for the sake of your friends and acquaintances who do have taste? But surely they don't all agree on what's attractive, so you can't please all of them, and you may even offend the sensibilities of the majority. I'm afraid this is leading us straight back to those abominable Joneses. Do people spend money for an interior decorator or landscape gardener just to show their friends they can afford to? But aren't there other ways to do this where the one who does the spending can get a little more fun out of it? Why not some diamonds or a yacht?

And what about the woman who is constantly re-covering a chair, a sofa, or maybe a whole roomful of furniture? Or is forever painting this or that or worrying over draperies? Or can't make up her mind where she likes this table or that armchair, and does such a continuous job of shifting that her house never looks the same from one week to another?

If she has plenty of time on her hands, plenty of money for paint and materials, and does all the work with a pleasant and relaxed feeling, then obviously it's a satisfying way for her to spend her time. I can think of nothing against it if she enjoys it and doesn't keep the house so constantly upset that it may be uncomfortable for the other members of the family. This woman's husband may find coming home at night much pleasanter if he can walk into the living room and see his favorite chair where it was last night, last week. Most people, I think, like to be conscious of stability. To find various things in a constant state of change in your home must be somewhat like trying to feel cozy in a busy railroad station. To everyone, perhaps, except the person who's responsible for the activity. For most of us a feeling of familiarity is comforting. How would you like to go home from your work every night to a different house? Even if each new home was a little more impressive than yesterday's, I don't believe you would care for it.

I can think of no sound reason for a layman to be interested in studying the stars except for that pleasant feeling of being able to recognize some of them when he looks up into the sky. There's good old Mars. Hello, Venus. Much more satisfying than just thinking, what a bright, pretty star! It's somewhat like accidentally running into an acquaintance in a strange town. And if you're in a foreign country and meet someone you know, you're simply delighted, even though he may be a person you might take a little trouble to avoid back home. To go out into our garden in the spring and find flowers we had never heard of would be exciting but it wouldn't be like greeting the old friends—crocuses, jonquils, tulips, lilacs.

And so I'm a little sorry for those people who often come home to a changed environment. Also, I'm not convinced that the one who is doing the changing is always in motion because she loves it; could it sometimes be restlessness or vanity? Or is she full of energy but unable to think of any other outlet for it? Or could it be that she doesn't much like her life and, wishing she could alter it, is determined to change at least a part of it, so she re-covers a chair or two and paints a yellow table green?

Some women are continually buying new things—or very old ones. I remember that the craze for antiques was raging when we moved to the country thirty years ago. A farmer's wife (she was in her upper eighties) who lived down the road from us had a house full of antiques overflowing into the cellar and attic, and it took her no time to find out that many people would pay almost any price for just any object if it was old enough. She also learned that few of them had any way of knowing whether or not the pieces were "authentic." She was a shrewd woman and, added to that, she thought all antique seekers were fairly ridiculous, so she bought all sorts of cheap odds and ends, using sense and discretion, and placed them around the house among her own possessions.

Many times an eager beaver would pounce onto one of these purchases and, assuming that it had been sitting there for a few generations, ask nothing but the price. And the old lady would name one far beyond what she had paid for the article and would make a sale. She was a religious woman, and if they had asked her about the age of the things she sold she would have told the truth. She cheated no one. If they wanted the hundred-year-old cradle or the week-old tray badly enough to pay the outlandish price she asked, let them have it; whichever they bought they seemed like fools to her.

But they weren't, really, if they were obeying some inner need, and not just behaving like sheep. Buy frantically if you truly enjoy it. On the other hand, live in a simple house if you would like to; don't go into debt for an elaborate one if you don't enjoy being in debt. Decide what you would like to do with the pennies you've saved through doing without the things that would give you no real satisfaction; make up your mind what you want to do with the time that is now yours since you began to snub Mrs. Jones.

I beg you to do as you please. If you want to bury your money under a rosebush, go ahead; it's *your* money. If you want to spend your leisure in a way least acceptable to the standards of others, please do; it's *your* time.

Have you, for instance, a sincere passion for flower arranging, or are you in a whirl about it only because everyone else is? I would never have known and couldn't have believed to what lengths that activity has gone if I hadn't done a good deal of talking to garden groups during the last few years. Like arranging furniture in a room, objects on a mantel, planning a flowerbed and the like, putting flowers in a vase can be done either to advantage or disadvantage. Some people are better at it than others, and I see nothing against trying to improve our ability; any gesture toward beautifying our surroundings seems to me worth while if it isn't overdone. But those of you who don't know about it would scarcely believe to what elaborate lengths garden club members go to in their efforts to outdo each other in the art of assembling flowers. Books and articles are written about it, classes are conducted and competitions arranged.

Here's the story of one competitive display I ran into, and it's not exaggerated. I was to talk to a club, and since I don't drive a car one of the members, as usual, called for me. She took me to the town hall, where the meeting was being held, and it happened to be exhibition day; we were early so we killed time by looking at the entries. They had already been judged and little cards by the vases told which arrangements had won.

There were many first and second prizes because there were various types of entries which competed only with others of the same type. I remember only two of these. One effort was to see who could do the most outstanding job of putting a single flower in a vase, and there were only two entries. The first prize was won by a woman who had put a Peace rose in a slender vase, and the second by a woman who had done the same thing. but the winner's vase was taller than the other and the stem of the rose a little longer. Both pretty and fully as effective as when I snip off a Peace rose and stick it in a vase.

The other group I remember had three entries; this was a miniature arrangement. I have forgotten what the two prize-winners looked like, but I thought the one that got no prize was by far the most attractive; I said so and my companion agreed.

"It is the prettiest, isn't it?" she said. "The judge liked it best too, but she said it didn't fulfill the requirements. It's just about one-eighth of an inch too tall for a miniature."

Well, I had heard about flower arrangers using tape measures, but I hadn't quite believed it. If we can't step back from a vase of flowers we've arranged and tell whether or not we like the looks of it without a tape measure to guide us, I can't quite grasp why we care *what* it looks like. It pleases us or it doesn't; isn't it as simple as that? But for the purposes of competition I suppose it isn't that simple; as you may remember, I don't happen to feel very friendly to competition in general.

My feeling, after I had looked at the two Peace roses and all the other entries and then at the lovely little miniature which was an eighth of an inch too long, was that all these goings-on might be appropriate for children up to perhaps the third or fourth grade, but after that age it would seem a bit too infantile.

I know a woman who might never get a prize in a flower-arranging contest, but if any flowers at all are in season there's always at least one beautiful bouquet in her living room which defies all tape measures; she has a gift for it. Once I was admiring one of her lovely arrangements and she said, "Oh, that bouquet isn't primarily for looks; it's because of their names. There isn't one flower there that hasn't a charming name," and she touched each blossom gently as she called the roll: Queen Anne's Lace, None-so-pretty, Lady's Delight, Bleeding Heart, Baby's Breath, Coral Bells, Fairy Flox, Forget-me-not, Heart's Ease. I have no prize handy for her, but she certainly deserves honorable mention; her name is Juanita Peck.

I suppose flower arranging could be called a hobby, and nobody looks down his nose at you for having one, and you probably aren't ashamed of yours, no matter what it may be, so why not make a hobby of, say, hanging on to your old car even if you *can't* open the windows by pushing a button. Anyway, the chances are that if you are too old and weak to open a car window all by yourself you're a menace as a driver and shouldn't be at the wheel.

Fred has a hobby which for a while threatened to develop

into a business. A friend had left some of her furniture with us temporarily, all of which we were welcome to use if we wanted to. One piece was a table, rather large but so light in weight that I could easily pick it up by myself. I used it for a desk and found it so handy that when she finally took it away I missed it. She had had it made; apparently it was impossible to buy that kind of table.

Fred said he would make me one, which surprised me, for when we needed the smallest job of carpentry done he hired a neighbor to do it. He did make the table and it was a complete success. This was a long time ago, and I'm not clear on the actual sequence of events but to put it briefly, if perhaps somewhat inaccurately, Fred decided to have half of our huge barn transformed into a woodworking shop. It consisted of a large, beautifully equipped workroom, a kiln, showroom, glue room, finishing room. A furnace was installed, and the outlay was several thousand dollars.

If you keep in mind that Fred had retired on a very small income and that, as far as I could judge, all this was done just in case I might want another table, I think you will agree with me that it was rather remarkable that I didn't so much as say mildly, "Have you gone out of your mind, darling?"

I'm glad I didn't say one discouraging word. Fred hasn't made any money from the venture, although some of the most exclusive shops from Boston to San Francisco have sold his creations, and still would be glad to, if he would make things for them. He stopped selling to shops long ago; the work was too confining, and if one is as particular as he is, and if all the overhead in a shop has to be charged against one man's output, there's no profit in it. For a year or two he worked very long hours, trying to fill orders, but when he had to compute the cost of a bowl, for instance, he had to figure his labor at less than he was paying a boy to mow the lawn. His things brought high prices from the point of view of the one who bought them but paid him too little. Which is, I've heard, true of all really fine handmade work.

However, this man I married who wasn't able (or inclined) to put up a pantry shelf, and who claims he failed in shopwork at school, has a top-rate standing in the field of crafts; at one time we were told by a director in a large art museum that Rossiter (that's my Fred) and Prestini were considered the two best wood turners in the United States. Fred has had a lot of recognition and has exhibited in a number of museums. His performance is gratifying, and his accomplishment and recognition are both desirable, but better than any of that is his enjoyment of the work. Recently he's been doing some hand carving, making some lovely pieces.

For me, personally, it's splendid; I've a cupboard full of most attractive bowls, plates, platters. I'm particularly fond of wooden dishes and in the early days, overcome by their beauty and by the fact that Fred had actually made them himself, I loved to take people into the showroom and see the looks of surprise and admiration on their faces when they saw a display which they hadn't expected.

Apparently I overdid it; one day, after some callers had gone, Fred said, "I'm glad you appreciate my genius, but when you take visitors into the showroom, instead of throwing out your arms and exclaiming over the magnificence, how would you like to let them do it?"

From then on I calmed down, outwardly at least. By now I'm almost blasé about it except that, having not the slightest artistic talent myself, I over-react to the ability of others in that field.

One of the countless things that impressed me after I got to New York (at the age of twenty-five) was the person who would look at a picture and say, for instance, "Oh, that must be Velasquez." In the first place, who on earth was Velasquez, and in the second, if my friend didn't recognize the picture, how could he possibly guess who had done it? It seemed like some occult power to me. For although I could recognize a literary style, it had never occurred to me that artists also had special styles.

I later met a woman who was as ignorant as I was about this and together we figured out that it was simply a matter of being familiar with the medium of expression, and we had better learn how to do it. So we went to the Metropolitan Museum and decided to concentrate on the pictures of only one artist that first day in order not to get confused. By chance we chose Corot.

We went again a week later and picked Rembrandt that day. The third visit we decided to review what we had perhaps learned, and undertook to wander around without the book to guide us to see if by great good luck we could spot either a Corot or a Rembrandt. Well, we recognized quite a few of both.

Neither one of us was particularly interested; we just didn't want to feel so ignorant in the presence of the geniuses who knew so much. My friend's own specialty was music and as for me, enjoyment through my eyes has always been one of my weakest points. So now we looked at each other and said, "If it's that easy, we're not impressed, and why should we bother with it?" So we stopped bothering.

However, I sometimes find myself wondering if I'm not missing something in my lack of appreciation of the art of painting, and vaguely try to do a little about it. One day I came across a reproduction of a modern painting and kept gazing at it, wondering if it was possible that it could mean anything to anybody. Then an old friend, an artist, came for a visit, and I showed her the picture and said, "I don't understand this *at all.*"

She gave the picture one glance, then replied in a pained voice, "Dear, do you *want* to?"

As a matter of fact, I didn't, particularly; if a thing doesn't appeal to us, must we try to force an interest in it?

If you have enough honesty with yourself and capacity for self-analysis to distinguish between what you do to please yourself and what you do to merely go along with others, and would keep a list for a few weeks of the hours and dollars you spend without getting any real pleasure and satisfaction in return, you might be surprised and perhaps a little concerned. It isn't helpful to our self-esteem to realize that we are a sort of mechanical toy which jumps when somebody pulls the string.

Let no one convince you that you are caught in the cogs of a wheel from which you can't escape. You can, if you care enough, and here are a few simple, definite things you can do.

One: if you go to an outside job and wish you didn't have to, you can do what I did when I was in my thirties: cut down drastically on everything that costs money. Get a part-time job and enjoy the extra hours.

Two: if you're uncomfortable unless you're wearing what everyone else is, hang your outmoded dresses in the back of the closet. They will be in style again some day.

Three: if you're at home all day, you can do many things to shorten your hours of labor. I've enumerated some, and you will think up others if you care less about what others think and more about what you really want.

Four: your friends and acquaintances won't drop in at any and all hours if you let them know you're allergic to it.

Five: if you like to belong to clubs, do so by all means, but if you don't, the safest thing is to say a simple no, thank you. Once you begin to explain why you don't want to join, some good talker will wear you down. And do your civic duty if you're so inclined, but don't let yourself be caught in more than you can do without feeling pushed one way and pulled another.

Six: you can, as I've already suggested, save time and energy by eliminating some of the meaningless social gestures and by handling the telephone nuisance more efficiently.

Seven: you can entertain more often those friends whom you really like to be with if you don't make too big a thing of it, and you can stop inviting and visiting the people who add nothing to your joy of life.

Eight: now act on your thoughts. If you truly want to simplify your life, you can. Keep in mind that you don't have to be a slave to anyone or anything, including your own second-hand values.

Even those who wear themselves out aping Mrs. Jones often speak disparagingly of her. Don't you? And yet, are you conforming? If you are, here is a thought guaranteed to give you a shock: you *are* Mrs. Jones. For she is you, and you, and you, who are permitting others to make your rules for you and run your lives.

XIV

When Evening Comes

IT SEEMS that almost nobody wants to die young and yet nobody wants to grow old either. Unfortunately, we have to do one or the other.

It is reasonable not to want to live through years of sickness, loneliness, uselessness at the end of our lives, and it's true that this is the fate of many people. However, instead of dreading it for ourselves, we can begin early to take steps toward avoiding it, steps which have already been suggested.

Some people hate the thought of old age in itself, even without the possible accompaniment of distress. This I cannot grasp. It is true that as the years pile up we lose some of the gifts of youth. Bubbling energy passes, but poise may come to make up for its loss. And a certain kind of ecstasy and enthusiasm fades; a girl of eighteen can get a tremendous thrill out of a party or a new dress, which is usually denied a woman of eighty.

To go back a little further, a child of one can become positively delirious with joy over beating a spoon on a tin pan, but few of us would care to stay at *that* early age, and neither would I choose to stay in my teens. Or the twenties or thirties. I like going forward, and what's wrong with still forging ahead after one has reached three score and ten?

Youth may get a lift out of feeling that one is captain of one's fate. But this doesn't work out, because fate includes quite a few things beyond our control. We can, however, learn to be captains of our souls, which is quite another thing and takes a long time; it is therefore something that only thoughtful living through many years can give us.

All this doesn't mean, of course, that I have a low opinion of youth. On the contrary, for me almost any beginning is exhilarating, whether it's that of a day, a book, a season, a play, or any project. And now I, who have always been at my best in the morning, find myself launched on the evening of my life. Yet I hardly notice it; none of the growing things around me are paying any attention whatever to the fact that I'm getting pretty far along, so I, too, ignore it.

It is March, and our little world is rubbing its eyes after a winter's sleep. Any morning now some redwing's call will waken me. Any evening the peepers will sing out the glad, gay news: spring has come! Crocuses are poking their little pointed noses through the mulch; like children playing in the snow they don't even notice that it's cold and windy and far from cozy.

You may have seen it any number of times in your life, but can anyone view calmly and indifferently this coming to life of things? The grass is deciding to be green again, jonquils are adding yellow to their costumes while crocuses are going in for more variety, yellow, white, various shades of lavender and purple. A little later tulips will abandon all restraint and will adorn themselves with every color they can think up, not caring how conspicuous they are as long as it's their beauty that makes them so.

Youth is rampant; things around me are in their morning, which makes me feel that I am too. And while they're busy growing I also get busy, planting flower seeds in the cold frame, lettuce, spinach, parsley, peas and onions in the garden, uncovering strawberries, digging parsnips, tossing mulch about. Adding my small contribution.

But what has the city to offer when spring shows up? Oh, plenty! The organ grinder plays *La Paloma*, boys swarm over the sidewalks playing marbles and little girls skip rope. When I lived in New York I liked to stop and watch them, sometimes even asking to take a turn at it.

I haven't lived there for thirty years; perhaps boys and girls and organ grinders are busy nowadays with other projects. But I feel sure that the grass, what there is of it, still turns green, and the trees put on leaves and the birds sing. And grown-ups have a newer, fresher look on their faces, even though it may be a brief one.

Spring is youth and is my favorite season, but when applied to human beings I don't go all out for it as many people seem to do. Youth may be refreshing, may have a certain charm, but to me it is also a little touching. Many young people are uncertain, feeling their way blindly, which is uncomfortable. Others are over-confident, too sure of themselves, and are headed for some downfalls, I fear. And, to put it bluntly, they are all a little raw.

It seems to me that if a very young person is a realist he insists on being somewhat bitter and callous along with it; a mature realist is simply sane, reasonable, honest. And so often the young idealist will go to extremes, then lean much too far the other way when he becomes disillusioned. And the suffering of youth, from a broken doll to a broken heart or a shattered ideal is acute and agonizing. As I look back I feel that I had an unusually happy childhood and satisfying youth, yet, up to the age of twenty-five or so, there were times when I felt that nothing but suicide was the answer to some particular problem. Not once since then.

Now summer comes, not a choice time in the hot city, and everyone who can escapes to beach or country. Here in Connecticut promises are now either fulfilled or broken; flowers and vegetables reward us for the pains we have taken or they go back on us. Our city friends flock to visit. The days are long, the pace eases up a little, and even if we aren't as exhilarated as we were in spring, summer is a welcome change.

And as we get into the summer of our lives we begin to acquire a little common sense, which is one of the most satisfactory qualities that a person could want. By then we know that the world won't come to an end if we come out second or even tenth best in some competition. We no longer even wish it *would* come to an end, and if someone disappoints us, we don't decide that there's no virtue in anybody at all. In other words, we have a little more balance than we had when we were twenty.

Then comes autumn, and those of us who are approaching the evening of life can perhaps learn a lesson. Do we have the idea that growing old is sure to be a little dull, maybe even ugly? The leaves on the trees have no such distressing notion; they haven't lived as many weeks as we have years, not much time to learn and no brain for thinking, yet they contrive to make their old age colorful and even, at times, startlingly glorious. Are we less than a leaf on a tree? Couldn't we strive to manage things so that those around us will enjoy us in our last years, rather than merely tolerate or pity us?

Finally the leaves fall to the ground, but their usefulness isn't over; if we gather them and put them on our gardens, they will decay and enrich the soil and aid a lettuce plant, a peony, a rose, a stalk of corn. I wouldn't burn the leaves if I were you; perhaps they like to make things grow and thus live on themselves.

But this is the time when humans begin to feel nervous about getting old. If a person is afraid of dying, I can vaguely understand his feeling; otherwise, it seems to me that the autumn of life is richer and more satisfying than anything so far. We've learned, surely, to take today's mishaps with a shrug, for we know that by tomorrow they will probably have lost their meaning. We can cope even with big troubles, for by now we have had enough experience with them to know that however devastating they may seem, it is impossible to suffer at top notch for long continued periods. So this, too, will pass.

And we have probably learned that money doesn't bring happiness and we are content with what we have. (I'm not of course talking about those who don't have enough to meet daily simple needs.) The Joneses have become quite absurd to us but we think of them with tolerance, minding only a little that there are still quite a few million people who pay tribute to them. We comfort ourselves with the thought that the human race is still in its infancy; it will grow up, as we have, and learn, unless the man in the moon becomes annoyed with us for trying to invade his territory and annihilates us, or unless we destroy ourselves with our own enchanting toys.

Autumn passes into winter, and I look forward to it with pleasure, with peace, quiet, a smoothly-running schedule; not a thing to interrupt me but the telephone, milkman, laundryman, postman, a neighbor, or maybe a blizzard which cuts off the electric power. With luck we might be snowbound without the power going off; there is no cozier feeling.

On winter mornings I write and answer mail. At twelve o'clock I go out of doors to get the sunshine vitamin and some oxygen. I may shovel snow, if it's dry and light to handle, or gather some fallen branches or cut up some minor logs in the protected sunny spot in front of the woodshed. After lunch I do a bit of housecleaning. By three o'clock I'm on the couch with a book and am still there at six when Fred comes in from the shop and pours the cocktails. Then to the kitchen to see about dinner.

Here we are in the winter of life; this is old age, looked forward to with dread by so many of us. With reason, too; we need only look around us to see how often it is accompanied by sickness and loneliness.

We have a great deal to learn about how to keep well. My guess is that our troubles come primarily from what our mothers ate and what we eat. After all, when scientists experiment on animals to find out what keeps them well and makes them sick, they don't, as far as I know, pay attention to daily baths, exercise, fresh air, eight hours' sleep, but to what the animals eat. Americans go overboard for the daily bath, but it's shocking what they will put in their stomachs. Until we learn what to eat and stick to it, we will probably be more or less miserable in the winter of our lives.

When I was in my early fifties I was at a dinner party one evening where all the others happened to be ten or fifteen years younger than I was; the topic of getting old came up, and each of us in turn chose the age he would like to be. To my surprise they all wanted to go back to somewhere around the late twenties and *stay* there.

My turn came last and I said, "Since I'm older than the rest of you, maybe you think I'm decrepit and can't bear it, so am lying to myself, but I don't want to go *back*, for goodness' sake! I've been fifty, now I want to see what sixty is like, and seventy, and eighty."

I still feel that way; I want to go forward. For some peculiar reason I have a picture of myself as a little old lady, sitting around in a cozy shawl, with someone bringing me my meals, and me smiling and doing nothing at all. I can't imagine how I managed to think that one up; I could happily stand that kind of life for only about fifteen minutes a day.

The best rule for living I know is to learn to live in the moment; nothing could be deader than the past and the future may never come. Not only may the trip you are planning for next month fall through because you are no longer alive to take it, but even the trip to the kitchen to get dinner may not materialize; you may slip on a rug and break your leg, and then someone else will have to do the cooking. (I'll omit the caustic remarks I could make about the custom of strewing rugs about on slippery floors.)

So the past is gone, the future may never come, for you; all you can count on is this present moment. It seems a big job, indeed, to build a happy life, but if we put our minds to it we can build happy moments, one right after another. Or at least pleasant ones, and the time will come when we're so in the habit of creating them that, lo and behold, we are having a serene and pleasant life, with fine prospects of it's lasting.

Now I'm not unrealistic enough to think that we can, merely by putting our minds to it, fill our lives full of only happy moments. And it's well that we can't; the person who doesn't, now and again, have to cope with trouble has little chance to learn patience and fortitude. But we can avoid unprofitable worry, we can refuse to think about misfortunes (our own and those of others) which we can in no way help.

When we are sad for some specific reason, such as the sickness or death of someone we love, there isn't much sense in trying to feel gay; however, we can try not to wallow in our misery. I once read that in time of sorrow every moment you can snatch out of the depths to enjoy something, whether a flower, a fragrance, or a cup of tea, will be of benefit to you, and I should think that might be true.

In times of depression, when I don't know why I'm feeling low, I prefer to weather it through rather than go to a movie, or go to visit somebody, or employ any of the other tricks which some people find helpful. I say to myself: perhaps it's just that my stomach's a little off, and in any case it will soon pass and I'll feel fine again; by tomorrow it won't make any difference that today I felt like biting everybody's head off, unless I indulge myself and make everyone around me uncomfortable; that would leave some kind of mark.

There are two things to learn and we can't start too early. One is to use each moment as it comes, the way a spendthrift uses money, paying it out gladly for our pleasure and profit. The other is to value it, as a miser does a dollar, by learning to put into it the sort of enjoyment that will stand by us straight through to the end.

What kind of enjoyment? Well, not material possessions, nor your physical attractions, nor fame, a hobby, a cause, love for individuals, doing good to others, nor even religion. Any one of these things, in one way or another, can fail you. Some of you may think that the last two would surely stand by you, but not necessarily. For the time may come when you no longer have the health or strength or money or incentive to do anything for anybody. As for religion, you might lose your faith. And even if you didn't, sitting around thinking about how nice it will be when you get to Heaven could become quite boring. And religion in its better sense, leaving everything to God and really trusting Him to do whatever is best for us, is comforting but must, I think, be accompanied by something more, unless a completely passive existence satisfies us.

And so what can we put into our daily lives that will see us straight through until the day we die? Nothing I can think of except a lively interest in the world we live in or in some part of it. This interest will differ with each temperament and will be constantly changing from one thing to another. Now it may be painting a table, ten minutes later perhaps something that has just happened in India. Or the opening of a new smash play. The amaryllis has a bud. This morning the milkman became the proud and happy father of an eight-pound boy!

The world abounds in events, from an onion seed which sprouted overnight to a new peace conference; it would seem a difficult task to lead a dull existence with so much going on. Our whole lives may be crowded with struggle, poverty, ill health, sorrow, but they need never be dull. And yet it seems to me that boredom is the most widespread curse through our last years.

We may lose many of our faculties, but as long as we have a clear mind we can think; some of us go through a long life without discovering how much pleasure we can get out of using our brains. Thinking may be a great boon to us when we're old if we have filled our moments with it through the years and have learned how to do it constructively rather than negatively.

Life has taught me that there are many undesirable things I need not submit to if I care enough to stand up against them. And I have also learned not to worry about nor struggle against the things I cannot change.

And I would say: be glad, above all, that you are obliged to work. There are two classes of people in the world: those who have to work in order to live, and those who never have had to. The second group is a small minority, I'm glad to say, for they are greatly to be pitied. There is a tremendous vacuum in their lives, for they can have no true understanding of the basic activity of all living creatures: the vital necessity of doing something in order to stay alive. I am grateful for many things, but perhaps most of all I am thankful that each morning when I get up there is work which I *have* to do.

And so in the winter of my life I want what I always have wanted: to work, to enjoy sixteen hours of every day and to sleep the other eight. I would like to keep my health, too, if it isn't too much to ask.

If the time should come when I can no longer work, if I lose my health, and if, for some reason beyond my control, I can't enjoy the days nor sleep at night, I hope I will have enough spirit left to accept my lot gracefully, since accept it I must. At long last, no other goal being possible, perhaps I will try to care what others think of my behavior; perhaps I will work hard at bearing my lot so bravely that those around me will say "Isn't she wonderful!" rather than "Isn't she pitiful!"

CPSIA information can be obtained
at www.ICGtesting.com
Printed in the USA
BVHW031604310321
603806BV00009B/1067